Improving Scottish
education

A report by HMIE on inspection and review 2002-2005

HM Inspectorate of Education 2006

HM Inspectorate of Education
Denholm House
Almondvale Business Park
Almondvale Way
Livingston
EH54 6GA

Tel: 01506 600 200
Fax: 01506 600 337
E-mail: enquiries@hmie.gov.uk

Produced for HMIE by Astron B40345 02/06

Published by HMIE, February 2006

Contents

Page

Note on Contents 1

1. Commentary by HM Senior Chief Inspector 2

2. Sector reports 7

   Pre-school 8

   Primary 22

   Secondary 34

   Special schools 46

   College 60

   Community learning and development 70

3. Major themes and significant issues 84

   3.1 School curriculum 84

   3.2 Achievement 86

   3.3 Learning 88

   3.4 Ethos and behaviour 89

   3.5 Meeting the needs of all learners 90

   3.6 Staffing, teaching and professional responsibility 92

   3.7 Leadership, change and accountability 94

   3.8 The national context: policy into practice 96

4. Improving Scottish education 100

Appendix: Note on evidence sources and the use of terms 104

Note on Contents

The Report

Improving Scottish Education comments on the quality of provision across all sectors and offers:

- a commentary by HM Senior Chief Inspector;

- a section with six summarising reports, each focusing on one of the sectors of education;

- a section summarising and commenting on some of the major themes and issues arising from the sector reports and other HMIE reports; and

- a final short section commenting on aspects which have led to overall improvement and indicating the focus of HMIE activities in the next few years.

Note: A number of 'signposts to improvement' are to be found throughout the report. Each focuses on a specific aspect and offers a number of pointers to what, in HMIE's view, promotes improvements to provision and outcomes for learners.

Website version

A web version of the report and other related materials is available on the HMIE website (www.hmie.gov.uk). This version comprises:

- electronic copy of the report with access to individual sections;

- all HMIE quality indicator data relating to inspections in each sector;

- summaries of stakeholders' views as gathered for primary and secondary sector inspections;

- a selection of facts and figures relating to each sector;

- information on national qualifications at secondary school level;

- some facts about the demographic context for Scottish education;

- information on the policy context for each sector; and

- a bibliography of HMIE and other reports, with hyperlinks.

Section One: Commentary by HMSCI

Scotland's young people and adult learners live and work in an increasingly complex and uncertain social, political, technological and economic environment. It is clear that the future will require a population with the confidence and skills to meet the challenges posed by fast and far reaching change. It follows that inspection must evaluate both how well today's needs are being met and the capacity of the education system to continue to improve. This report, therefore, not only evaluates current performance but also considers how ready we are to meet future challenges.

Inspection evidence shows that Scottish education does many things well and some things particularly well. Most learners are well supported and well taught. The quality of service provided at the pre-school stage is strong overall, and most children are given a very positive start in their learning. In primary and secondary schools, young people generally make sound progress in their learning, behave well, have good relationships with their teachers and ultimately achieve an appropriate range of formal qualifications. Provision for children and young people with additional support needs in mainstream and special schools allows many to make considerable progress in their personal and social development. Parents report high levels of satisfaction about their children's schooling. Teachers are also positive about their own work despite its often challenging nature.

Beyond school education, our college sector has responded very well to new demands, showing flexibility and creativity in matching the needs of learners, employers and the economy more generally. Staff in community learning and development are also making an increasingly effective contribution to improving the life chances of some of our most vulnerable young people and adults and to building capacity in communities more widely.

International comparisons provide a broadly positive view of the performance of our young people. Over the period of this report our pupils have generally performed well in PISA[1] studies undertaken by OECD. Performances of our 15-year olds in reading, mathematical and scientific literacies were among the top third of all countries which participated (32 participated in 2000, 41 in 2003). Encouragingly, the gap in performance between high and low attainment in Scotland had narrowed in some aspects in the 2003 survey to a greater extent than in other countries.

Scottish education is also recognised internationally for its pioneering work in quality improvement. The 'Scottish approach' to combining internal and external evaluation, based originally on *How good is our school?* and now extended to further education and community learning and development, has attracted worldwide interest for the way in which it uses quality indicators as a common language to help identify strengths and areas for improvement. The very positive response of schools, authorities and other education providers to that approach is much to their credit and places them at the forefront of quality improvement internationally.

---

[1] *Programme for International Student Assessment 2000* and *2003* (OECD : Organisation for Economic and Cultural Development)

These are real strengths to build upon as we improve education further. At the same time a number of long-standing problems remain evident and some fresh issues emerge from our inspection evidence.

While many of our young people perform well in school and beyond, too many do not develop sufficiently the competences, capabilities and values which are vital for the future success and well-being both of themselves and of Scotland as a whole. For many, that future success will depend on participation in learning once they leave school, and our colleges and community learning and development play a key role in that process. However, over 20% of adults report difficulties with literacy and numeracy and too many young people aged 16 to 19 are not in education, employment or training. That is a loss both for the individual concerned and to society more widely. Ultimately the success of all of our young people will depend on their readiness for learning and on the ability of our teachers to encourage high aspirations and to stimulate, sustain and support an interest in learning which will endure beyond the passing of an examination. Critically, we need learning and teaching of the highest quality, and ways in which that quality can be enhanced are developed throughout this report.

Although primary and secondary schools are generally providing a curriculum in line with existing national guidance, the future context requires a reappraisal of the content and extent of that guidance. The review currently being undertaken by the Scottish Executive following *A Curriculum for Excellence* is therefore both necessary and timely. Its recognition of the critical role of education in developing our young people as successful learners, effective contributors, confident individuals, and responsible citizens provides a unique and powerful opportunity to address some fundamental issues.

As part of the review the following areas need to be addressed.

- Clarity is required about those elements which should form part of every young person's education, irrespective of perceived ability, social background or school attended.

- There is a need to be much more rigorous and explicit about the development and certification of essential skills, particularly literacy and numeracy. This requirement goes beyond pupils with specific difficulties to *all* pupils, including those entering higher education.

- Space is needed for imaginative teaching which can capitalise on approaches which make learning relevant, lively and motivating.

- 'Vocational education', often seen as an alternative to 'academic education', must be integral to the education of all pupils. The aim must not be simply to seek 'parity of esteem' between two separate types of education but to provide an appropriate education for all. Central to that task should be a much greater emphasis on creativity and the application of learning and on making clear the relevance and importance of what is being studied.

- A more pronounced focus is required on health education.

- A clearer and more consistent approach is required to education for citizenship and the key role of schools in transmitting values.

Future success will require an education system which is itself responsive and flexible and which is open to new ideas and new approaches to learning and teaching. That, as always, will depend crucially on the quality and commitment of our teachers in all sectors. Inspection findings show that the overall quality of teaching is high. It is particularly pleasing to note, in general and including through inspection of aspects of initial teacher education, the quality of so many of those entering the profession. Scotland is fortunate in having a highly professional teaching force. It is essential that this professionalism includes embracing innovation, taking responsibility for personal performance and development, and encouraging and supporting each young person as an individual. While it is not yet possible to evaluate the long-term impact of *A Teaching Profession for the 21st Century*, its focus on the professional role of teachers is of critical importance.

Education authorities can and should make a key contribution to improving quality in schools. Our inspections have identified much good practice in authorities which is clearly adding value to the work of schools. However, there is considerable variation in performance across education authorities and some have much work to do to match the standards of the best. We will be publishing a report shortly which will address this issue directly.

The central importance of high-quality leadership has been a consistent theme in inspection reports over many years. Over that time the demands on our education leaders have grown and the work of our best headteachers, college principals and education officials bears comparison with leaders and managers in any walk of life. However, as yet, we have not seen sufficient improvement in leadership overall. We are still reporting important weaknesses in leadership across all formal education sectors. Inspection evidence shows that one of the most powerful keys to success lies in high-quality and determined leadership which is creative, sets high expectations, focuses on learning, stresses the importance of meeting the individual needs of learners, and promotes and supports teaching of the highest quality.

Inspection reports on a significant number of pre-school centres, schools, colleges and other providers show evidence of important weaknesses. In too many cases there is an unacceptable variation in the quality of learning and teaching across classes. Encouragingly, actions taken following inspection or review are bringing about positive, and in some cases very substantial, improvement. However, some problems or weaknesses are deep-seated and may appear intractable. It is essential that any such problems are identified at an early stage and necessary action is taken before they can impact so directly on the learners involved. Scotland's commitment to self-evaluation must go beyond diagnosis to ensure that necessary action is taken and real improvement achieved.

We have increasing evidence about the factors which make learning effective. However, we must also recognise that many of the factors associated with poor performance lie outside the centre, school or college attended, limiting the readiness of some young people for learning. The need for establishments and teachers to work effectively with parents and carers and with all those services which support young people and their families remains vital. Traditions, structures and even values present real challenges to joint working but our inspections suggest a much needed and growing determination to find effective ways forward.

Since the *Standards in Scotland's Schools etc (2000) Act*, the Scottish Executive has been more explicit about expectations for the education system. It has also provided substantial increases in funding to address some fundamental weaknesses in provision. Sets of national priorities covering different sectors have been largely successful in broadening the educational agenda, and their impact is identifiable at different levels in the system. The policy framework set in *Ambitious, Excellent Schools* and *Learning Through Life; Life Through Learning* provides a context within which many of the issues raised in this report can be addressed. However, the number and variety of national and local initiatives represents a considerable challenge to those who provide education and sensible prioritisation has been difficult to achieve. It is important that current efforts to create greater coherence and reduce complexity are effective and sustained in order that energies and resources can be channelled to where they can make the greatest difference.

For our part, HMIE must ensure that inspection meets best value criteria and makes the maximum impact with minimum intrusion. We have already streamlined our inspection and review models and will continue to examine ways of making the process as a whole more efficient. In particular, we are working with other inspectorates to develop an integrated approach to inspecting all of those services which support young people and their families. Our more focused inspection approaches have been well received and are already showing positive results. The challenge for inspection and other systems of accountability is to promote creativity and well-judged innovation without losing focus on standards, quality and effectiveness.

A main theme of this report is the need to build on the undoubted strengths of our education system to meet the challenges of an increasingly complex and uncertain future. That will require a greater determination to address long-standing problems associated with underachievement and a recognition that future success will require greater flexibility and creativity in our approaches to learning and teaching. Our systems of assessment, certification and accountability must also recognise and reinforce these new purposes. The kind of learning embodied in the emerging curriculum must be reflected directly in the qualifications which our young people gain as they move through and beyond the school and in the measures we use to judge effectiveness.

This report is designed to promote continuous improvement in Scottish education. It poses challenges for everyone involved if a culture of high expectations, high achievement and high quality is to be the norm and if the system is to embrace the kind of flexibility and ambition which future success demands.

GRAHAM DONALDSON

Pre-school

Primary

Secondary

Special Schools

College

Community Learning and Development

HMIe

improving Scottish education

Section Two: Pre-school sector

1. Features and overview

1.1 The pre-school sector

The experience of early childhood in Scotland in the early part of the 21st century has, in many ways, changed quite dramatically from that experienced by previous generations. Partly as a result of the huge increase in the number of families with working parents,[2] many children will now spend a significant portion of the pre-school stage outwith the family home. Most children now spend some part of the week being cared for and educated in a pre-school setting in which their parents will not normally be present. There is a wide variety of such settings including:

- education authority nursery schools or nursery classes attached to primary schools;

- nursery classes in the independent school sector;

- private nurseries;

- playgroups in the voluntary sector; and

- providers from any of the above groupings offering 'wrap-around care' for children at times outwith the conventional educational day.

The proportion of children receiving pre-school education is now at an all-time high, representing virtually universal coverage. Every three and four year old in Scotland is entitled to a free, part-time placement in pre-school provision. In January 2004, almost 160,000 children under five years of age received pre-school education or formal childcare. In 2005, 81% of three year olds and 98% of four year olds attended pre-school education. This places a great responsibility on those who deliver pre-school provision to ensure these young children are offered the highest quality of care and education. Pre-school education is no longer an optional extra, but rather it is now a standard stage in the educational journey of virtually all Scotland's young learners.

Scotland's pre-school providers are generally very successful at ensuring that children are very well cared for. In most cases, they also ensure that children engage effectively in their learning and make a sound start across a range of important areas. Children generally learn to work and play well with other children in pre-school centres, and they do so in settings which are characterised by fun and enjoyment. Some improvement is needed, however, in the quality of talk and interaction between adults and children to ensure that all children's learning needs are met fully. In a significant number of centres, particularly in the private and voluntary sectors, the quality of leadership and of other factors dependent on leadership need to improve.

Inspections in this sector are undertaken jointly with the Care Commission.

---

[2] see Appendix for use of terms

1.2 Key strengths

Though pre-school education is delivered in a variety of settings and contexts, certain strengths are common to many centres. These include:

- close relationships between pre-school staff and parents which help ensure effective attention to children's pastoral needs;

- the commitment of staff, and the increasing number who have qualifications;

- the effective organisation and use of learning envrionments in many centres to promote purposeful play and independent learning;

- the range of interesting learning opportunities and activities available to children;

- consistently good progress of children across key aspects of learning and development; and

- secure, confident and motivated children who display an interest in learning.

1.3 Aspects for improvement

While the sector is characterised by these common considerable strengths, there are also some important areas within which improvement is required.

Leadership: The quality of leadership needs to be improved, particularly in a substantial proportion of centres in the private and voluntary sectors. Across all pre-school settings, managers/headteachers should more consistently focus their leadership directly on improving the quality of children's learning and the skills of staff in promoting it.

Learning: Staff working in the pre-school sector need to improve how they:

- address the learning needs of individuals, particularly with regard to those who require additional support in their learning;

- engage directly with children to extend their understanding and learning; and

- use information gathered on children's learning to promote their future progress.

2. Key outcomes

Introduction

No formal national standards for attainment are used at the pre-school stage. However, children's progress is monitored against a common framework of experiences in the five key aspects of development and learning as illustrated in *A Curriculum Framework for Children 3 to 5* (Scottish Executive/Learning and Teaching Scotland). Children's progress is assessed through procedures established by the centre itself or by an education authority or other governing body.

2.1 Children's progress in development and learning

Overall, children in the pre-school sector achieve well in a broad range of important outcomes. Pre-school centres are strong on valuing children as individuals and celebrating their individual achievements. The level of progress made by children in pre-school offers a sound basis upon which primary school staff can build. In less effective centres, the amount of choice provided in aspects of children's learning can be insufficient to allow them to develop skills in independent learning and making decisions.

CHILDREN'S PROGRESS IN DEVELOPMENT AND LEARNING

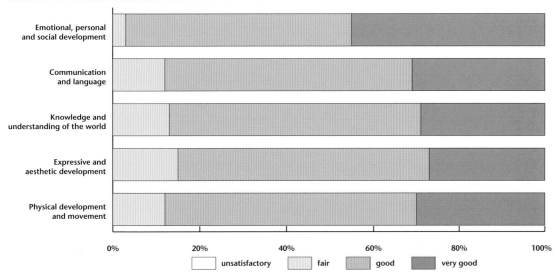

Distribution of quality indicator evaluations in the pre-school sector, 2003-2005.

In **emotional, personal and social development,** progress is often very good. Most children adapt well to established pre-school routines. Their experience of learning through play engenders great enthusiasm and motivation for learning. Children frequently have fun while learning. They learn how to co-operate with a number of adults and other children, a factor crucial to future development in learning and in life. Parents regularly comment on how well their child's confidence and self-esteem develop through their pre-school experiences. Centres are also generally successful in helping to foster children's curiosity and creativity, encouraging them to follow their own interests at a pace which suits them as individuals.

>> Signpost to improvement in early writing development

Awareness of contexts for writing and development of writing skills can be encouraged through children:

- *practising making letter shapes in the sand;*
- *drawing stories;*
- *labelling artwork; and*
- *pretending, in play situations, to write shopping lists, take telephone messages, write emails, read menus, write greetings cards.*

In **communication and language**, most children develop important skills in listening and talking. Most learn to listen well and respond appropriately to instructions from adults. They gain confidence in talking and listening in one-to-one situations and in small group discussions. Centres are increasingly effective at developing interest and aptitude in early literacy activities. Most children develop an interest in, and a basic understanding of, books and stories, and many begin to understand simple features of text. While a minority also make a start to developing simple writing skills, their progress in acquiring and developing appropriate skills in early writing is too often limited. Where this happens, children's interest in the range of contexts for writing is insufficiently stimulated and developed.

In **knowledge and understanding of the world**, children develop an interest in, and knowledge of, numbers and shapes, often through informal activities. In most centres, the local environment is used effectively to promote learning. Through visits to parks and gardens children learn to reflect on nature and the world around them. Increasingly, they are learning to use a range of ICT equipment in their learning, including making independent use of computers, listening centres, digital cameras and programmable toys. Most are also developing an awareness of cultures other than their own. In some centres, however, children do not have consistently good opportunities to develop skills of observation and investigation. In others, too much emphasis on adult-directed activities limits their opportunities to encounter and solve problems in their learning.

To promote their **expressive and aesthetic** development, children in pre-school provision are often surrounded by opportunities to express themselves. They learn to express their imagination and feelings through painting, modelling and role-play activities. Their concentration levels grow and develop. Through the richness of opportunities for role-play in particular, they develop understanding in a whole range of important areas, including communicating and co-operating with others. There remains more scope, however, for improving the extent to which children's interest in aspects of expressive and aesthetic development is harnessed to ensure that they develop appropriate skills progressively. While, for example, most children are making good progress in the technical skills of art and craft, they are not always encouraged to express themselves freely enough. Children's capacity to express themselves fully in musical experiences also requires further development in many cases.

In **physical development and movement**, most children learn to be creative and self-challenging through exploring the range of movement of which their bodies are capable and taking part in energetic, physical play. Most also learn about the need for safety during play. Increasingly, children are learning about positive attitudes to healthy diet and healthy living. Children's natural need to move freely, to learn about the capabilities of their bodies and to take part in energetic exercise is, in some instances, restricted either by available space or by a lack of challenge provided by adults. Also, children sometimes lack skills and confidence in using large play equipment.

2.2 Stakeholders' views

HMIE and the Care Commission do not formally collect the views of children as part of their inspection procedures. However, through completion of the pre-inspection questionnaires, parents are asked whether their child enjoys being at nursery and whether their child is treated fairly by staff. In almost all cases, parents responded positively to these questions.

Signpost to improvement in ‹‹
energetic physical play

Opportunities each day for children to:

- experience energetic play on large equipment indoors and outside;
- use space indoors and outside to run, jump, skip, climb, move to music, dance;
- learn about the world of energetic activity outside their playroom; and
- enjoy physical activity outside in all weathers.

3. Meeting the needs of all children

>> **Signpost to improvement in adult/child interaction**

Staff:

- *engage in frequent, systematic reflection on how, why and when adults interact with children to develop their learning;*
- *establish agreed approaches;*
- *apply these approaches while children are playing and learning;*
- *take children's needs and preferences into account; and*
- *provide regular and constructive feedback to children, encouraging them to reflect on their own learning.*

3.1 Children's learning experiences

The quality of children's learning experiences in pre-school depends both on the nature of the opportunities offered to them and on the ways in which adults interact with them to promote and extend their play and learning. Overall, staff who work with pre-school children are caring and committed in their approaches. They usually know children well as individuals and quickly establish positive relationships with them. In most centres, the quality of interaction between adults and children is good, with staff demonstrating skilled questioning and a willingness to take account of children's contributions in discussion. In some centres, staff are clearly very skilled in helping children understand and develop through well-timed and purposeful interaction with them as they play and learn. This is rooted in a clear understanding of how children learn effectively.

However, this high level of skill in promoting children's learning is not consistently evident in all centres. Too often, in centres in which learning is not well managed or organised, staff lack sufficient skill in supporting, developing or extending children's understanding. In a few centres, the pace of children's progress in their learning is not given high enough priority or is not well monitored. The learning needs of more able children should be more clearly identified. Staff also need to agree and apply approaches to addressing these needs. In cases of weak practice, the level of challenge in children's learning is not sufficient to help them make steady progress.

3.2 Quality of programmes

The principles of the pre-school curriculum are now well established across the country and provide the basis for a coherent experience for children. National guidance is generally well used to plan, organise, assess and support learning activities. While the experiences provided for children are appropriate overall, not all centres are sufficiently skilled in tailoring this curriculum to the learning needs of particular groups and individual children who need additional support.

CURRICULUM AREAS

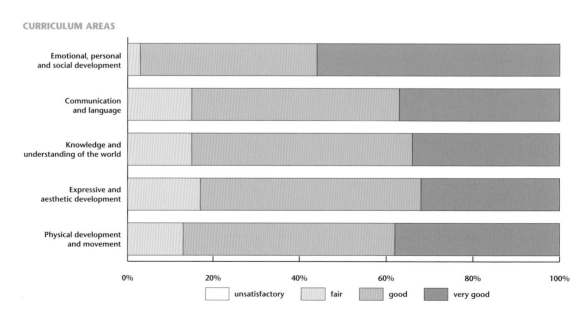

Distribution of quality indicator evaluations in the pre-school sector, 2003-2005.

Aspects of programmes which inspectors generally find to be strengths include:

- the breadth of experiences across a wide range of areas;

- approaches to the curriculum and learning which encourage all children to enjoy their learning experiences;

- the opportunities provided for children to exercise choice in many centres;

- the extent to which different aspects of the curriculum are delivered in integrated ways which respond to children's interests and experiences;

- the quality of experiences in emotional, personal and social development; and

- the development of experiences which give increasingly effective emphasis to how children can learn to work co-operatively with others, and to live healthily.

A number of aspects of curricular programmes feature relatively frequently as areas of weakness. In implementing and adapting *A Curriculum Framework for Children 3 to 5,* some centres try to provide for all areas of the curriculum at all times of the day. In some cases, for example where accommodation is restricted, this can lead to a superficial provision which affords children little scope and depth to their learning opportunities. In a minority of centres, the balance between allowing children to select freely from the activities provided and ensuring that all children have a broad range of learning experiences requires further attention. In a few centres, staff do not ensure that children's experiences are rooted in contexts which fully stimulate their interests.

Signpost to improvement in ‹‹ the curriculum

- *Improvements to the curriculum are rooted in a shared, clear understanding and rationale.*

- *There is a strong focus on what children need to encounter in their learning and in their life.*

- *Staff take as their starting point children's knowledge, competences and interests and skilfully mould a 'learning package' which is designed to meet the needs of groups and individuals.*

›› Signpost to improvement in meeting all children's needs

- *Staff have high expectations of, and aspirations for, all children in their learning.*
- *Staff are determined to adapt activities to meet the individual learning needs of each child.*
- *A spirit of open collaboration is developed with a range of agencies to monitor and support individual children with identified additional needs.*
- *There is active encouragement for the involvement of all who have a stake in the child's development in planning to address children's needs.*
- *Careful attention is paid to monitoring the progress of children with additional needs, including the involvement of parents, wherever appropriate.*
- *Staff ensure that parents of children with additional needs have a clear role in helping to support their child in his/her learning.*

3.3 Climate and support

In over two out of every five centres inspected, **support for children's development and learning** was very good. Inspection evidence indicates that staff quickly establish close and effective relationships with parents. In most centres, key members of staff take responsibility for co-ordinating the learning of allocated groups of children. Staff very effectively keep parents updated on aspects of how children react to different experiences, often on a very informal basis, and they communicate regularly with them on pastoral issues. Staff also now increasingly display and share planned learning programmes with parents, although the extent to which parents are involved as full partners in their child's learning and development is inconsistent. Centres need to encourage parents to contribute to assessing their child's learning, bringing important information and insight from the home and other contexts.

Staff in an increasing number of centres now work closely with a range of agencies to improve the quality of support available for children. Where this is most effective, it is very well co-ordinated and involves parents appropriately.

Increasingly, staff make effective use of **individualised educational programmes (IEPs)** as a planned way to address additional support needs and to record the progress made as a result. In a small minority of cases, staff have started to use personal learning planning as a way of organising children's learning. This is used for all pupils and is a mechanism to help staff to focus support on individual need. In a growing minority of centres, parents are increasingly involved in the process of formulating, delivering and reviewing agreed learning targets for their children. In some centres, however, IEPs and other learning plans lack sufficiently detailed targets to promote children's progress. Monitoring of progress against learning targets too often lacks rigour.

Overall, there is a need for greater consistency across the sector with regard to the identification of children's learning needs, particularly in the voluntary and private sectors. In a minority of centres, even when learning needs have been identified, staff are not sufficiently clear on what steps should be taken to ensure appropriate progress. In less effective practice, staff need to take more active steps to seek the assistance of other agencies to support children in their learning, and they need to ensure closer and more active involvement of parents in the process. Approaches to ensuring support for children in transferring to primary education, though often strong in pastoral aspects, do not always give sufficient attention to continuity and progression in children's learning. Implementation of *A Curriculum for Excellence* will provide an opportunity to address these issues and improve coherence in children's experiences across the pre-school and early primary school years.

The **environment for learning** is clearly influenced to a very significant extent by the physical environment and accommodation available. In the pre-school sector, the range and variety of accommodation is particularly wide. Amongst voluntary providers, it frequently includes use of village and church halls. In most centres the layout of playrooms in the available accommodation is designed with children's learning needs to the fore. In these instances, a stimulating range of resources which reinforce children's desire to learn increasingly involves a variety of technology, including computers. In the majority of instances, activities on offer to children are wide-ranging yet carefully planned to extend interest and learning. In those centres where this works well, children's views will have been taken into account in how the learning environment is laid out. In these cases, it is clear that the playroom is designed for those whom it is intended to serve: young children.

>> *Signpost to improvement in the learning environment*

- *Staff ensure that the environment supports experiences suited to the needs of individual learners.*
- *The physical environment invites children to learn and allows them to access readily all available resources and experiences, as appropriate.*
- *The physical environment is organised to allow daily opportunities for children to engage in energetic physical movement.*

However, some common weaknesses are evident in the learning environment. Poor quality accommodation, or ineffective management of accommodation, is an issue in a small minority of centres. This can result in an environment which is not wholly appropriate for children's learning. In a few cases, space is simply too limited to allow children to experience a balanced and active learning programme. Staff do not always take good account of children's needs and they sometimes provide an environment based on insufficient understanding of what a play environment should be like. In such provision, how adults organise the layout of the playroom can reduce the quality of children's learning.

At times, resources are either too limited or are inappropriate to the needs of children. In weak practice, a predominance of displays created primarily by adults undermines the value of children's contributions. In a few centres, the availability of facilities for high quality and challenging energetic play (indoor and outdoor) is too restricted.

4. Leadership and capacity to improve

4.1 Leadership

LEADERSHIP

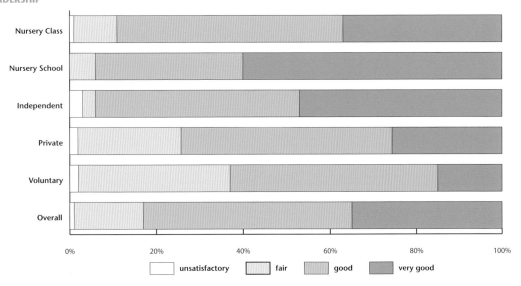

Distribution of quality indicator evaluations in the pre-school sector, 2003-2005.

In just over a third of centres inspected, the quality of leadership had major strengths. In a further half, leadership had more strengths than weaknesses. Generally, evaluations of leadership are centred on the contribution of the headteacher[3] or centre manager. In larger provision, increasingly, leadership is defined by the combined contribution of senior managers within a nursery or centre.

Common areas of strength in management and leadership include the following. Most headteachers/managers:

- display clear commitment to the well-being of the children in their provision;

- work to ensure that relationships with parents are very positive;

- recognise the importance of a positive ethos and a happy, constructive learning environment for children;

- are committed to ensuring a broad and balanced curriculum which allows children to select from a wide variety of learning experiences; and

- recognise the value of effective staff teamwork, seeking to ensure that all staff are involved in decisions which affect the life and work of the centre.

---

[3] see Appendix for use of terms

In too many cases, however, inconsistencies and weaknesses are evident in key aspects of leadership. There were significant weaknesses in about one in seven inspections, although this was very variable across the different types of provider. Leadership had weaknesses in a notably larger proportion of centres in both the private sector (around one in four centres) and in the voluntary sector (around one in three centres). In almost all cases the key weakness was that improving children's learning was not sufficiently well prioritised. Characteristic of such ineffective practice is:

- poor strategic leadership;

- an over-focus on administration and daily routines, often at the expense of a commitment to improving children's experiences;

- insufficient attention to ensuring high-quality learning experiences for children;

- a lack of clarity about management roles and responsibilities; and

- a tendency to work in isolation from other professionals and agencies, including education authority staff.

4.2 Capacity to improve

Where leadership is well focused on improving children's learning, staff reflect effectively on practice and they plan appropriately for future improvement. In a small but growing number of centres, the views of staff, parents and, occasionally, children, are taken into account prior to drawing up priorities for improvement. In such high quality practice, senior managers monitor a range of key areas, including written plans on what children will learn, as well as records of children's progress. In a few centres, senior managers carefully monitor and review the quality of staff interaction with children, providing helpful, constructive feedback to staff. Importantly, managers and staff also carefully monitor and review the quality of experiences offered to individuals and groups of children. How children learn and how staff can improve this learning is the key focus. In all of these examples, the principal motivation in undertaking these activities is to help to improve the quality of provision and, ultimately, the experiences of children.

Overall, the quality of monitoring of children's learning experiences and the quality of self-evaluation more generally are still too inconsistent across the sector. In a significant minority of cases they are notably weak. In such instances, there is a lack of commitment amongst staff to genuine and productive professional reflection on their practice.

Well-founded approaches to evaluating how staff interact with children to help develop their learning and progress are too infrequently established. Often, the views of parents and children are not considered in drawing up priorities for further improvement. In a minority of cases, improvement plans are too general and insufficiently rooted in careful evaluation. As a result, priorities do not always focus sufficiently on measures which will lead to improvement in children's learning. In such cases staff monitoring of progress towards implementation of identified priorities is often uneven and, overall, lacking in rigour.

The pre-school sector is characterised by great commitment from staff. This commitment to children now needs to be matched by increasing attention to the quality of leadership, closely focused on children's learning, and to how centres self-evaluate to plan for future improvement.

Signpost to improvement in ‹‹
leadership and
improvement

- *High-quality leadership for learning ensures that all staff focus clearly and consistently on what, and how well, all children learn.*
- *Managers and headteachers ensure that staff receive clear feedback on their performance in leading and supporting children's learning.*
- *Where relevant, education authorities ensure that high-quality staff development is available to managers and headteachers.*
- *Where relevant, education authority staff ensure regular and sustained support for, and challenge to, centres to ensure that all children make appropriate progress in their learning.*
- *Self-evaluation is rigorous and leads to improved outcomes for children.*

Section Two: Primary sector

1. Features and overview

1.1 The primary sector

In most primary schools in Scotland in 2005, pupils are taught by one class teacher for at least a year. In smaller schools, the same teacher may lead a class for up to seven years. Pupils follow a broad curriculum informed by national guidance.[4] The class teacher is responsible for finding out, understanding and meeting pupils' pastoral and learning needs. The teacher will share that role on a day-to-day basis with others such as classroom assistants and visiting teachers.

Directly underpinning the work of the class teacher is the leadership within the school and from the education authority. Traditionally, the role of leader has rested, almost exclusively, with the headteacher. This varies from the teaching headteacher in a small primary school to the largest schools with a management team which includes several depute headteachers and, more recently, principal teachers. As schools embrace continuous change and improvement, relevant aspects of leadership are increasingly being shared by a range of staff.

In the period covered by this report, primary schools responded to a range of opportunities and challenges resulting from a number of pieces of legislation and policy initiatives, each of which required school staff to review their expectations and improve their knowledge and skills. The entry into P1 of pupils with at least one year of pre-school education, and a stronger emphasis on earlier interventions to support pupils, have altered teachers' expectations of what pupils in the early stages of primary can achieve.

Overall, staff in primary schools have a good track record in making sure that pupils' pastoral needs are well met, resulting in pupils who are well looked after and happy to be at school. Their effectiveness in meeting the learning needs of all pupils is more variable. The generally good quality of learning and teaching and of leadership in most schools provides a secure basis for further improvement.

---

[4] 5-14 Curriculum and Assessment in Scotland National Guidelines; National Priorities for school education

1.2 Key strengths

Key strengths of the primary sector include the following:

- well-motivated pupils who remain keen to learn all the way through primary school;

- the quality of pastoral care, shared with parents, which enables pupils to feel secure and ready to learn in school;

- a supportive climate for learning and positive relationships between staff and pupils;

- a curriculum which entitles all pupils to a broad range of learning opportunities;

- skilled teaching staff who are committed to doing the best for pupils;

- the contribution made by support staff to pupils' care and learning;

- the attainment of pupils from P1 to P4; and

- high stakeholder satisfaction with almost all aspects of the work of schools.

1.3 Aspects for improvement

This report identifies the following key themes as aspects for further improvement in primary education.

Learning: The quality of pupils' learning experiences is still too variable and too often lacks relevance, engagement and excitement. How pupils learn and acquire a range of skills enabling them to achieve greater independence as learners across their seven years in primary school requires further development.

Achievement: Pupils can achieve more than they currently do. This is particularly relevant to:

- pupils at P6 and P7; and

- lower-attaining pupils whose subsequent learning and life chances depend heavily on the quality of their learning and achievement in their primary years.

Leadership: Strategic leadership with a clear focus on learning and teaching is required. All staff need to accept that they have a leadership role to play in building the school's capacity for improvement so that the needs of all learners are better met.

Primary 2

2. Key outcomes

Introduction

Overall, pupils in primary schools achieve well across a broad range of areas. They are developing a good range of knowledge, understanding, skills and attitudes through their classwork and their interactions with others in their daily school lives. Details about their attainment and achievements in specific curriculum areas, including strengths and points for improvement, can be found in HMIE reports on English language, mathematics, science, Gaelic, and modern languages. A summary of some key points relating to English language and mathematics follows.

2.1 Attainment in English language and mathematics

In **English language**, most pupils:

- attain very well from P1 to P4;

- attain better in reading (81% attaining national levels) than in writing (74%);

- are able to listen to, and follow, instructions and explanations, most commonly given by adults, and can contribute effectively to discussions led by adults; and

- read regularly for pleasure and can discuss with adults features of books they have read.

However, overall attainment in English language in about one quarter of schools inspected has important weaknesses. Pupils' overall strong attainment at P1 to P4 is not sustained through to P7. Nationally collated data show that boys' attainment in both reading and writing is lower than that of girls from P3 onwards. By P7 almost a half of all boys are not achieving expected levels in writing.

In **mathematics**, most pupils:

- attain very well at the early stages with almost all pupils in P3 achieving appropriate national levels and an increasing number achieving these levels earlier than might be expected;

- are attaining well at the middle stages with most pupils in P4 attaining appropriate national levels but only a very small percentage (3%) exceeding these;

- in P6 (82%) are achieving or exceeding appropriate national levels, with just over 20% of pupils in P6 exceeding them;

- have well-developed skills in written calculation; and

- have a good awareness of a range of shapes and can interpret data from graphs of appropriate complexity.

However, there are important weaknesses in overall attainment in about 20% of schools. At P7, only 70% of pupils are attaining the appropriate level, with 15% exceeding it. While there has been a small increase in the number of pupils attaining the appropriate level at P7, 30% of pupils are leaving primary school without doing so.

2.2 Broader achievements

Inspectors[5] found that pupils:

- are developing good social skills which also enable them to work well with others;

- can perform to an audience showing skill in aspects of the expressive arts;

- are increasingly engaging successfully in enterprise activities;

- are developing a good understanding of the need to live healthily and safely;

- are developing an understanding of citizenship, rights and responsibilities;

- have a growing awareness of sustainability issues such as caring for the environment; and

- are developing an understanding of what it means to be Scottish and are extending their awareness of other world religions and issues relating to the diversity of cultures.

While pupils are developing a range of skills in areas such as citizenship and enterprise there is still substantial room for further improvement. As yet, their opportunities to contribute to discussions about learning and teaching are too limited. Almost all schools offer opportunities to develop interests and aptitudes through a range of extra-curricular clubs and activities.

2.3 Stakeholders' views

- **Pupils**: Almost all pupils thought that the school helped them to keep safe and healthy and that teachers expected them to work as hard as they could. Over a quarter did not think that the behaviour of pupils in their school was good.

- **Parents**: Almost all parents thought their children enjoyed school and were treated fairly and that they themselves were made to feel welcome, while almost a fifth did not think they had a clear idea of the school's priorities for improvement.

- **Staff**: All staff thought they cared effectively for pupils and that teachers set high standards for their attainment. Over a quarter of support staff did not think they had good opportunities to be involved in school decision making.

---

[5] See Appendix for use of terms

3. Meeting the needs of all learners

3.1 Learning and teaching

Most pupils in primary schools are highly motivated and keen to learn and this is sustained from P1 through to P7. They react positively to a varied range of effective learning approaches. This can be seen, for example, in their responses to the ways in which mental mathematics is taught or in the ways they respond to good formative assessment. They adapt very well to the use of ICT and sometimes grasp potential uses before their teachers do.

Given these very positive factors, schools are not always clear enough about how best to develop the pupil as a learner. Schools may be achieving good success in supporting progression in programme content for pupils from P1 to P7 but have not applied similar thinking to ensuring progression in **pupils' skills as learners**. As a result, many pupils have not developed high-level and independent learning skills by the time they leave P7. For example, a pupil in a P3 class may develop very good skills in working collaboratively with others and achieve good outcomes and success from doing so. The same pupil may then enter the P4 class and not use these skills at all then go on to P5 where the teacher may decide to 'introduce' collaborative group work.

The commitment and skill of teachers is a recurring strength. Almost all are committed to doing the best for their pupils and to ensuring that they benefit from educational opportunities arising from initiatives such as early intervention approaches. For the most part, teachers have good relationships with pupils and make good use of praise to build pupils' self-confidence and reward their achievements. Many teachers have a growing repertoire of effective **teaching approaches** which they can adapt to meet pupils' learning needs. Examples of these include direct interactive teaching and learning in mental mathematics, collaborative work in writing and drama and an increasing use of technologies such as interactive whiteboards. Evidence emerging from schools where teachers have been involved with national projects[6] designed to improve the quality of learning and teaching shows that, where approaches have been successful, this has energised and motivated teachers. In particular, the formative assessment project within the *Assessment is for Learning* programme has helped many teachers integrate good assessment practice into their day-to-day teaching. In the most effective examples, pupils have a clear understanding of what they are trying to learn and what is expected of them.

**Signpost to improvement in ‹‹
independent learning**

By P7 pupils should have developed good skills as independent learners. Features of growing independence in learning are that pupils:

- *know how to work with others;*
- *can decide when to work alone and when to collaborate with others;*
- *respect and value the ideas and opinions of others;*
- *know how to seek help and where to find information;*
- *know what questions to ask and have developed independent research skills;*
- *can think creatively and solve problems on their own and with others;*
- *can communicate orally and in writing on their own and with others;*
- *can set their own goals and plan and organise their own work;*
- *can use available time well;*
- *can use ICT effectively in a range of learning activities; and*
- *can evaluate their own strengths and areas for improvement.*

THE TEACHING PROCESS/PUPILS' LEARNING EXPERIENCES

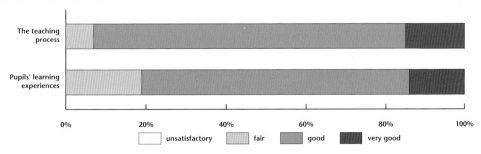

Distribution of quality indicator evaluations in the primary sector, 2002-2005.

---

[6] e.g. Assessment is for Learning – project 1; Building Bridges in Literacy; *Determined to Succeed*

>> Signpost to improvement in learning and teaching

- Relationships between teachers and pupils are positive and productive and conducive to learning.
- There is a clear focus on meeting pupils' learning needs.
- Teachers engage pupils in high-quality interactions designed to extend their thinking.
- Pupils' learning experiences are stimulating and active.
- Pupils become more engaged with their learning, see its relevance, and experience success.
- Teachers have a wide repertoire of well-understood approaches and can use and adapt these effectively.
- Pupils gain increasing independence as learners as they progress through school.
- Teachers and pupils are engaged in dialogue about evaluating and improving the process of learning and teaching.

In the 15% of schools where the overall quality of teaching is evaluated as very good, staff have worked together, under positive leadership, to improve the quality of learning and teaching in their own classrooms as well as ensuring that they share best practice and use common, consistent approaches across the school. Very good teachers are typically very reflective, able to evaluate and alter their own practice and are, themselves, good learners.

Teachers need to ensure that learning is a vibrant activity which is not over-directed by them. They need to extend pupils' thinking through talk and interaction with them and through opportunities for pupils to work co-operatively with other pupils. **Learning activities** should be relevant to pupils' lives and build on their needs, interests and prior knowledge from home, school or the community. Improvements which could be made include more varied and more imaginative use by pupils of ICT in their learning, a quicker pace of learning and learning activities which are better matched to pupils' motivation and levels of need. This is most evident at P6/P7 where too often pupils are doing 'more of the same'. Teachers' expectations of what pupils can achieve, particularly at the upper stages of primary, are not yet consistently high enough and opportunities for pupils to express views about and discuss their learning experiences are infrequent.

3.2 Curriculum

A key strength continues to be the breadth of the curriculum offered to pupils. In almost all primary schools the curriculum is well structured. Schools are using the national 5-14 curriculum guidelines to offer breadth and consistency of experience for all. Since 2001 they have used the national priorities and other initiatives such as health promotion and enterprise education to extend learning opportunities for pupils. Programmes of study which aim to ensure the progressive development of pupils' skills are most well developed in mathematics and English language. There have been significant improvements in programmes for science. Skills such as problem solving or literacy are not well developed across the curriculum.

Many schools have found it difficult to balance maintaining a broad curriculum following existing national guidance with the creative adaptation of the curriculum to meet all pupils' learning needs. Those needs may relate to opportunities for some study in depth, for greater choice, or for time to explore the same learning points through different contexts. Some schools do not make best use of the 20% of time available for local flexibility in the curriculum. Very few schools have a well-developed rationale for how they use this 'flexibility time' or have evaluated the impact of their decisions on pupils' achievements.

Teachers have consistently reported that the maintenance and development of the detail in current curriculum guidelines and the related expectations for assessment were proving to be increasingly challenging to deliver. In November 2004, Scottish Ministers responded to the National Debate[7] by making a commitment to *'streamline the existing guidelines to free up space for more challenge and enjoyment, and to help to raise attainment'*.[8] The resulting *A Curriculum for Excellence* will offer opportunities for schools to review the extent to which their curriculum responds to the values, purposes and principles proposed and to make appropriate improvements.

3.3 Climate and support

In almost all schools, staff have established a positive climate for learning. Typically, staff and pupils identify strongly with their school communities and have very good relationships with each other. Although the quality of **accommodation** varies, staff make good, and often imaginative, use of the accommodation which is available to create stimulating and supportive environments for learning. Pupils are happy to be at school and attendance levels are high. Staff often set high expectations for pupils' behaviour and their application to work and, overall, most pupils respond very well. Most schools promote a strong sense of equality and fairness. Most work hard to ensure that all pupils are included socially in school. Many are developing good skills in identifying the needs of pupils from a variety of ethnic backgrounds such as asylum seekers and children of Gypsy Travellers. Increasingly, pupils are involved in making decisions about some aspects of their school lives.

In almost all schools, the positive ethos, the quality of staff-pupil relationships and involvement in activities within and beyond the school day promote pupils' **personal and social development** (PSD) very well. In the best situations, focused programmes for PSD help pupils to develop their understanding of personal and social issues and to reflect on their own relationships with others. However, the range of skills taught can lack progression and the goals of the programme may not be mirrored in the broader work of the school or in its involvement in the life of the community. For example, if pupils learn about issues such as race equality, anti-bullying, disability or healthy living, they need to see what they are learning about practised in the day-to-day work of their schools.

---

[7] National Debate on Education, 2002

[8] *A Curriculum for Excellence – Ministerial Response*, November 2004

The quality of pastoral care is an area of major strength. Staff meet pupils' care and welfare needs very well and links with parents in this respect are strong. Almost all schools have appropriate procedures in place for child protection. Approaches for supporting the pastoral aspects of transition for children from pre-school to primary and from P7 to secondary are usually well-established and effective.

CLIMATE AND RELATIONSHIPS/PARTNERSHIP WITH PARENTS, THE SCHOOL BOARD AND THE COMMUNITY

Distribution of quality indicator evaluations in the primary sector, 2002-2005.

Within the context of consistently high-quality **pastoral care** and an overall positive climate for learning, there are areas which require greater vigilance. One area of concern is the very small but important number of pupils who, despite good efforts on the part of school staff, manage to 'slip through the net' of care and achievement. A common example is the pupil who has frequent absences, and whose learning needs as a result are not adequately met. In such cases, where there can be child protection concerns and the involvement of other agencies, it is crucial that school staff develop their skills as proactive partners in order to make sure that children get help when they need it. Another area of concern is the impact of the behaviour of a few pupils on their own learning and on the overall perceptions of a significant number of pupils about behaviour in their schools. In more than a quarter of primary schools there is room for improving the management of a few pupils who present with behaviour problems. For the most part, this manifests itself as low-level indiscipline. In a small number of classes the behaviour of a few pupils is unacceptable.[9]

Schools are strengthening their **links with staff from a range of professional agencies** such as police, speech and language therapists, psychologists, social workers and health professionals as part of the move towards more integrated community schooling. In some cases, links focus on well-established partnerships to provide services for all children. Examples of these include joint working in safety education, crime prevention, health screening and health promotion. Increasingly they focus on ensuring high-quality support services for vulnerable children and their families. Although links are generally effective, there are instances of strained relationships and weaknesses in communications between other agencies and staff in schools.

---

[9] *A Climate for Learning: A Review of the Implementation of the Better Behaviour, Better Learning report* (HMIE 2005)

Overall, the learning needs of pupils with clearly defined **additional support needs** are well met. Most schools ensure that pupils with additional needs are well included with their peers and are making good and sustained progress in their learning. Teachers work well with support staff and parents, and with specialist agencies where needed, to identify and address pupils' learning needs. This often includes the effective use of individualised educational programmes and high quality, regular one-to-one or small group teaching and support. A range of support staff in schools such as classroom assistants and additional support needs auxiliaries provide good support for pupils on a day-to-day basis and contribute significantly to their learning and overall progress.

MEETING PUPILS' NEEDS

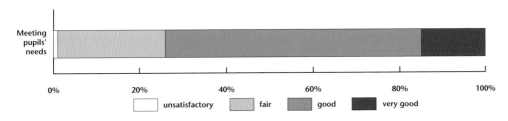

Distribution of quality indicator evaluations in the primary sector, 2002-2005.

Most teachers are effective at meeting the needs of pupils who have clearly defined learning difficulties. For example, many schools are successful in their work with pupils for whom the early stages of learning to read is difficult. These same schools may be less effective at adjusting curricular and teaching approaches to meet the learning needs of some other groups of pupils. They may need more effective approaches to extend pupils' reading skills or to meet the interests of underachieving boys or to challenge high-achieving pupils for whom English is an additional language. Too often the learning needs of more vulnerable pupils such as looked after, and looked after and accommodated, children are overlooked while their pastoral and care needs are addressed.

Schools' partnerships for meeting the broad range of pupils' learning needs are not yet sufficiently well developed. This is often underpinned by a lack of clarity as to who leads whole-school approaches to learning and teaching and a limited understanding on the part of staff about relevant good practice in addressing learning needs. In particular, partnerships with parents about pupils' learning, and between teaching and support staff, have much potential to be extended. At points of transition, such as from pre-school to primary, from stage to stage within primary or from primary to secondary, teachers pay considerable attention to pupils' pastoral needs. They are less effective in ensuring that learning activities result in a continuous experience for pupils and take account of the need for a progressive development in their knowledge, understanding and skills.

Signpost to improvement in << meeting the needs of all learners

- *Pastoral care and personal and social development have the goal of ensuring that pupils are successful as learners.*
- *In schools where there are very real daily challenges in making sure that all pupils are included, staff maintain a clear focus on the quality of pupils' learning and achievement for all.*
- *Schools have a clear and shared commitment to equality and inclusion for all, well-thought-out approaches to learning and teaching and a strong ethos of self-evaluation and improvement.*
- *Schools have clear strategies in place to ensure that lower-attaining pupils are supported to progress at a pace which will bring their attainment closer to that of their classmates.*
- *Staff are skilled in working together and with a range of partners, including parents, to support and engage pupils in learning.*
- *Staff use a range of tools, such as individualised educational programmes, effectively.*
- *Schools use curriculum flexibility effectively to meet pupils' learning needs.*
- *There is a 'pool' of expert knowledge within the school and its partners about the range of specialised needs presented by pupils.*
- *Programmes and learning activities for personal and social development are relevant and regularly updated to address pupils' needs.*

4. Leadership and capacity to improve

4.1 Leadership

The overall quality of leadership is good (44%) or very good (39%) in most schools. For the most part this evaluation reflects on the effectiveness of the headteacher. Increasingly, however, evaluations of leadership take account of the role of all staff in leading aspects of improvement and, where appropriate, include the role of the education authority.

Most headteachers are very committed to the well-being of pupils and the effective management of their schools. Where relevant, they work well with other promoted members of staff such as depute headteachers and, more recently, principal teachers to ensure that all areas of the school's work are well managed. They establish a positive ethos and good relationships within, and beyond, the school community. They have established good links with professional agencies such as social work and educational psychology to enable them to support the pastoral and learning needs of pupils. Increasingly, headteachers are developing their skills in inter-agency working in order to learn from and work with others, more effectively to meet the needs of all pupils. Most headteachers create conditions which enable good learning and teaching to take place.

However, in about 20% of schools, there are important weaknesses in leadership. The most common are:

- lack of vision, strategic thinking and direction;

- poor relationships with staff and other partners;

- lack of focus on, and engagement in, learning and teaching; and

- limited understanding of how to develop the school's capacity for self-improvement.

LEADERSHIP

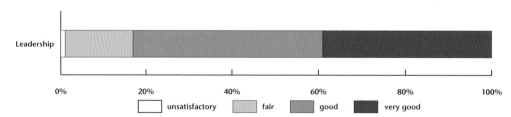

Distribution of quality indicator evaluations in the primary sector, 2002-2005.

4.2 Capacity to improve

In most schools, headteachers establish good quality teamwork amongst staff and engage staff, to varying degrees, in evaluating the work of the school. Most headteachers have developed a variety of tools which they can use to evaluate the work of the school. These include: discussing plans with teachers and offering feedback; formal or informal classroom observation; sampling pupils' work; tracking pupils' progress; and seeking stakeholders' views. Most headteachers support staff development and enable staff to attend courses usually linked to priorities identified in the school's development plan.

The most effective headteachers work with staff within a climate of continuous improvement. Their joint efforts are focused on improving the quality of pupils' learning. In these situations, teachers reflect on their own practice and the practice of colleagues. They learn from the constructive feedback of colleagues which includes senior promoted staff. Senior staff support and model effective teaching. In the very best situations, pupils contribute to feedback on the quality of learning and teaching.

In over a third of schools, **self-evaluation** has important weaknesses. Some headteachers may use a range of approaches but without a clear understanding as to the overall purpose and intended outcomes. Staff may not be engaged in or committed to the process of self-evaluation and perceive senior management activities in this area as a threat or of limited usefulness. There is often not a clear enough focus on learning and teaching. Too often schools do not consult effectively with all staff, pupils, parents and other relevant stakeholders about key decisions affecting pupils' learning and achievements. Where this happens, the outcomes of self-evaluation may have limited impact on practice and on the experiences of pupils.

Overall, the primary sector is well placed to secure further improvement. Pupils achieve across a broad range of areas and standards of attainment are good. Leadership is effective in most schools but is not yet sufficiently focused on the quality of learning and teaching in classrooms. The commitment and teamwork of staff is a strength. *A Curriculum for Excellence* presents a major opportunity for further improvements. This challenges all primary schools to improve the quality of the curriculum and the quality of learning for all pupils. This report highlights specific areas of strength and the directions that headteachers and staff need to take to meet that challenge.

Signpost to improvement in leadership «

- Headteachers develop a shared vision for the future and a clear sense of direction.
- Learning and teaching is placed at the heart of the work of the school.
- Expectations of what staff and pupils can achieve are high.
- Vision and creativity are used to ensure that staff focus on both the quality of <u>how</u> pupils achieve as well as <u>what</u> they achieve.
- There is a strong emphasis on meeting the needs of learners and a shared understanding of how children learn best.
- Staff, parents and pupils are regularly involved in dialogue about school improvement.
- Parents and other stakeholders are engaged in the business of learning.
- Senior promoted staff engage directly in learning and teaching.
- There is commitment to the continuing professional development of all staff, which includes a clear focus on the teacher as learner and good quality opportunities for teachers to learn from each other.
- Staff receive systematic and sustained support and constructive feedback as individuals and teams.
- Feedback is based on a thorough and shared knowledge of current good practice within and beyond the school.
- Staff share in the leadership of learning.

Section Two: Secondary sector

1. Features and overview

1.1 The secondary sector

Scottish pupils normally complete at least four years of secondary education until they reach the minimum school leaving age of 16. Over 65% of young people choose to stay at school for a fifth year, and around 45% of the original year group also complete a sixth year. During their time at secondary school, most pupils study a broad range of subjects in S1/S2, from which they select around eight main subjects to take in S3/S4. They then specialise in four or five areas in S5/S6.

Pupils receive a range of support[10] for their personal and social needs and advice about future career paths. Many experience the world of work. Large numbers of pupils participate in a broad range of out-of-school activities including sport, music and drama, residential experiences and educational visits. Many schools offer visits abroad and exchange visits where pupils play host to students from other countries. Personal and social education offers support in developing pupils' understanding of themselves, including a range of health issues and how they relate to others.

At the end of S4, most pupils take national examinations, mainly at Standard Grade, although increasingly in other national qualifications (NQs). At the end of S5, most pupils take a further set of national examinations, including Highers, which remain the main point of reference for university entrance. At the end of S6, pupils may take further examinations at Higher, Advanced Higher or other levels.

In the period covered by this report, secondary schools responded well to a range of opportunities and challenges resulting from national and local initiatives, each of which required school staff to review their expectations and improve their knowledge and skills.

The vast majority of schools are seeking ways to become more effective. National priorities for school education have successfully focused attention on developments in areas such as creativity, enterprise and education for sustainability. In addition, recent developments in curriculum flexibility have begun the process of improving the quality of learning and achievement for a number of pupils, notably the lower-attaining. Now, in the context of *A Curriculum for Excellence*, secondary education needs to review its aims and approaches. Schools need to focus more effectively on the broader achievement of all young people, and in particular on the attainment of those in S1/S2, boys, the lowest-attaining groups and vulnerable children.

---

[10] When inspecting secondary schools, inspectors also examine the work of units attached to and managed by the school, which provide support for pupils with additional support needs. They thus comment on the school's success with all pupils. This sector report takes a similar approach.

1.2 Key strengths

Key strengths of the secondary sector include the following.

- Pupils perform well by international standards.

- Many schools have a high level of pastoral care and a positive ethos, which help to encourage pupils' motivation.

- Most teachers are skilled in their subject or aspect and are committed to their pupils.

- Many headteachers have a particularly positive impact on the life of their school as a community.

- Stakeholders are broadly satisfied with almost all aspects of the work of secondary schools.

1.3 Aspects for improvement

This report identifies the following key themes as aspects for further improvement in secondary education.

Successful learning for all: The main focus for improvement in secondary schools should be on improving learning by engaging, challenging and motivating all young people better, and encouraging in them a greater sense of responsibility and independence. In doing so, schools should ensure that there is high quality in pupils' learning experiences in every class and greater consistency in the quality of those experiences across the school.

Achievement: Secondary schools need to ensure success for all pupils and gauge that success against a broad set of aims. These should include:

- improving performance at S1/S2;

- improving qualification levels;

- improving the performance of boys;

- addressing the needs of lower-attaining pupils;

- increasing pupils' self-confidence and ability to collaborate in achieving success; and

- increasing pupils' awareness of their potential contribution to their community and environment.

Leadership: A major focus for leadership in future should be on developing leadership at all levels with a strong drive on improving learning and teaching.

Responsibility and accountability for improving the quality of service: Schools should take greater ownership of and responsibility for improving the quality of the education service they provide, and should recognise their accountability to all stakeholders. They should increasingly be able to demonstrate the value they are adding for all learners, including the difference they make to all young people's achievements. Staff at all levels should fulfil their individual and collective roles in the objective evaluation of the quality of learning, and take action to meet learners' needs more effectively.

Secondary 2

2. Key outcomes

Introduction

Attainment in examinations is an important measure of the extent to which learners are successful. Many schools also provide a wide range of activities which considerably enhance the formal timetabled curriculum and which promote the development of broader achievement for those who take part.

2.1 Attainment

When evaluating the overall quality of attainment in a school, inspectors consider pupils' performance in the context of the school and the quality of education provided. The proportion of schools in which the overall quality of attainment at S1-S4 is fair or unsatisfactory remains too high. The picture at S5/S6 is more positive.

OVERALL QUALITY OF ATTAINMENT

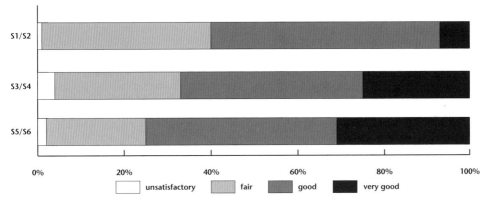

Distribution of quality indicator evaluations in the secondary sector, 2002-2005.

At S1/S2, standards in reading, writing and mathematics rose steadily over the period 2001-2004. The rise was less notable in writing, where just over half of the pupils attained the appropriate national level. The proportion of pupils attaining the appropriate national level in mathematics was around 60%. Girls performed better than boys in all of the above areas. By the end of S2, an increasing proportion of pupils reached level F, the highest level in the 5-14 framework, in reading and mathematics. More broadly, Scottish pupils perform notably better than the international average in mathematics and science.[11] In most schools, beyond reading, writing and mathematics, pupils' standards of attainment are not monitored systematically or benchmarked against national levels. As a result, schools are not well placed to report on pupils' progress across much of the curriculum. Inspections show that the overall quality of attainment at S1/S2 is variable across schools and subjects. They also show that teachers do not build consistently on prior learning and that pupils are often under-challenged.

---

[11] Trends in Mathematics and Science Study (TIMSS) of 2003 – an international survey which measures performance at P5 and S2. Forty-six countries took part in the 2003 survey at S2

Scottish pupils aged 15 perform significantly above the OECD average in reading, mathematical and scientific literacies when set against the performance of other countries.[12] In the last few years, almost all pupils have succeeded by the end of S4 in attaining five plus awards at SCQF[13] level 3 or better and most at SCQF level 4 or better. Around 35% have attained five plus awards at level 5 or better. Pupils' performance at these levels has remained largely unchanged over the 2002-2005 period. Girls continue to perform consistently better than boys. The proportions of pupils attaining one or more, three or more or five or more awards at SCQF level 6 by the end of S6 has shown no significant improvement. Again, girls perform better than boys. Performance at SCQF level 7 also shows no significant improvement.

The average attainment of the highest performing group of pupils has increased slightly over the period. However, the performance of the lowest 20%, as measured against national levels and examinations, has remained static. Around 60% of looked after, and looked after and accommodated, young people who are 16 to 17 have gained no qualifications at SCQF level 3 or above. Some of these young people gain awards in courses at colleges of further education, through extended work experience, and in activities accredited by voluntary organisations. Few of these awards are sufficiently recognised in the current range of school and national measures of success.

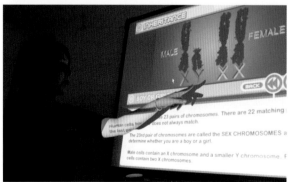

[12] Programme for International Student Assessment (PISA) of 2003
[13] **Scottish Credit and Qualifications Framework (SCQF) levels:**
7: Advanced Higher at A-C; CSYS at A-C
6: Higher at A-C
5: Intermediate 2 at A-C; Standard Grade at 1-2
4: Intermediate 1 at A-C; Standard Grade at 3-4
3: Access 3 Cluster; Standard Grade at 5-6

Secondary 2

2.2 Broader achievements

The learning experiences in secondary schools aim to develop a range of learning skills and positive attitudes to work. Over the last five years, schools have placed an increasing emphasis on encouraging and recognising young people's broader achievement. Some subjects include opportunities for learners to develop skills in independent learning and in aspects such as ICT and research. Many schools develop well pupils' awareness of the need to adopt a healthy lifestyle. Most schools offer a range of activities beyond the formal curriculum. Some activities, for example in the context of education for work, enterprise and community service, enable pupils to develop self-confidence, an understanding of their rights and responsibilities and of their role as citizens, and a sense of personal ambition. Where pupils participate in these kinds of activities, the experience also improves the school's ethos and pupils' engagement with the life and work of the school. The challenge for schools now is to aim for full participation. Increased uptake of The Duke of Edinburgh's Award Scheme, eco-school activities and other initiatives such as the Prince's Trust, and youth programmes accredited by the Award Scheme Development and Accreditation Network (ASDAN) also have a positive impact.

While key outcomes for the sector have been measured largely in terms of performance in examinations and against national levels, we are still at an early stage in tracking, recording and giving recognition to pupils' broader achievements.

Several education authorities have tried to evaluate schools' performance in areas such as pupils' involvement in sport, or buddying schemes. However, there are no national benchmarks to measure meaningfully the wider achievements of pupils. Schools and education authorities require better support for more systematic monitoring of these aspects, and to measure and improve their impact on young people.

2.3 Stakeholders' views

- **Pupils**: Almost all pupils thought that teachers expected them to work as hard as they could and that teachers explained things when they were having difficulties. Most also felt that they were helped to stay safe and healthy. The areas of least satisfaction amongst pupils related to the behaviour of other pupils, the extent to which they were treated fairly in the school, the effectiveness of staff in dealing with bullying, and the extent to which pupils had a say in how to make the school better.

- **Parents**: Almost all parents felt that their children enjoyed school and were treated fairly and with care. They felt that parents' evenings were helpful and informative and school reports gave them good information about their children's progress. They felt schools were well led and that teachers set high standards for pupils' attainment. The area of least satisfaction related to the extent to which parents had a clear idea of the priorities for improving the school.

- **Staff**: Almost all staff were satisfied that pupils' successes were regularly celebrated, that schools communicated clearly to parents the standard of work they expected and that they dealt effectively with any instances of bullying. The areas of least satisfaction related to the lack of opportunity to be involved in decision-making processes, and the extent to which indiscipline was dealt with effectively or consistently in the school.

3. Meeting the needs of all learners

3.1 Learning and teaching

>> **Signpost to improvement in learning and teaching**

- *Review the effectiveness of existing learning experiences in the context of the purposes of education as defined by the four capacities from A Curriculum for Excellence.*
- *Increase the relevance of pupils' curriculum experiences.*
- *Provide learning activities which build on previous success, adopting an appropriate pace, and giving more challenge and responsibility to pupils.*
- *Introduce more collaborative approaches, engaging pupils more actively in thinking about their learning and requiring them to think creatively.*
- *Enable teachers to have professional discussion about effective learning and teaching, including observing colleagues' good practice.*
- *Build an ethos founded on secure and positive relationships between teachers and learners.*

Most secondary teachers are committed, demonstrate good knowledge of their subject and are generally skilful in their planning for lessons and in their explanations of subject ideas to their pupils. For the most part, they create a positive learning environment, are supportive of pupils and make good use of praise. The majority use a range of approaches and activities to motivate learners. Most pupils respond well to the positive climate in class and are attentive and on task. Teachers increasingly use well-focused direct teaching with clearly explained learning outcomes, sound questioning and discussion. Teachers need to ensure they encourage pupils to take more responsibility for their own learning, for example through independent tasks and collaborative activities. Some schools have introduced approaches where the ongoing use of assessment is central to the learning process. These approaches have significant potential to improve the quality of learning. Teachers' use of ICT is also increasing and is most effective where they have identified the specific role it should play in lessons. Too often, however, ICT resources are not being used effectively, even where they are readily available.

Increasingly, and recently within the context of *A Teaching Profession for the 21st Century*, schools have deployed a range of additional staff who support the work of teachers. Such staff, along with other groups of personnel, provide a good service. Schools should ensure that support staff are appropriately included in decision making and receive relevant and high-quality staff development.

THE TEACHING PROCESS/PUPILS' LEARNING EXPERIENCES/MEETING PUPILS' NEEDS

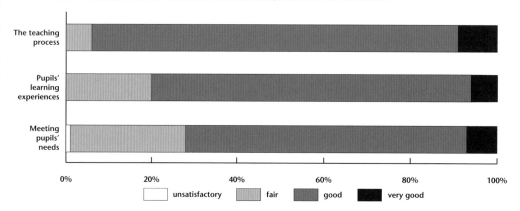

Distribution of quality indicator evaluations in the secondary sector, 2002-2005.

Most teachers have a broad level of knowledge of the strengths of their pupils and of how their learning is progressing. However, some teachers do not make sufficient use of information about individuals' performances and current rates of progress to provide appropriate learning experiences. Some schools have grouped pupils according to their prior attainment in some subject areas. This approach has made a contribution to meeting the needs of many pupils, but only where the make up of such groups is flexible, assessment information is used effectively to guide learning and care is taken to avoid lowered expectations from both teachers and pupils in some classes.

3.2 Curriculum

Secondary schools make good use of the information transferred from their associated primary schools about pupils' pastoral and support for learning needs. However, too many do not make effective use of information about pupils' prior learning and previous rates of progress. Schools should continue to improve this aspect of their work.

In the context of current curriculum arrangements, most pupils study a broad range of subjects in S1/S2, from which they choose around eight subjects in S3/S4, before specialising in four or five in S5/S6. While these arrangements generally serve pupils well, they do not always meet fully the needs of all. *A Curriculum for Excellence* has recently clarified the purposes of the curriculum. Schools should review their approaches to curriculum flexibility and choice to ensure that all learners achieve success. Schools are placing an increasing focus on cross-curricular issues and the development of areas such as enterprise and citizenship, often in response to national initiatives such as *Determined to Succeed*[14] or the national priorities for school education. Schools have been largely successful in implementing a curriculum with qualifications covering a number of levels, following the introduction of new national qualifications.

An increasing number of schools are introducing more flexible approaches and alternative curricular experiences for some pupils. In the majority of cases, improved approaches include a significant element of vocational education, mainly for pupils in S3/S4 who are not attaining well in the context of their current curriculum. In some cases such approaches increase pupils' motivation, particularly where part of their studies takes place in a college context. While some schools provide appropriate experiences for pupils in preparation for their future study and work, others have yet to promote such opportunities for all pupils. Other types of flexible approach have entailed changes to pupils' curricula or to the stage at which they take national qualifications. In a number of cases, changes are well considered and appropriately monitored and evaluated, and lead to increased motivation. At times, however, changes are introduced without adequate preparation or sufficient consideration of the potential effects on pupils' learning and future opportunities. In addition, schools have sometimes sought to provide alternative experiences or programmes without sufficiently considering how pupils' current

STRUCTURE OF THE CURRICULUM

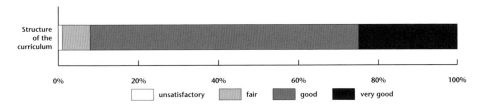

Distribution of quality indicator evaluations in the secondary sector, 2002-2005.

---

[14] *Determined to Succeed* (Scottish Executive, 2002)

experiences and programmes could be improved. Educational gain for pupils as a result of curriculum changes is, in a considerable number of cases, as yet unclear. The introduction of *A Curriculum for Excellence* will provide all schools with the opportunity to consider the extent to which their current curriculum arrangements promote the values, purposes and principles advocated for all learners.

The majority of schools provide appropriate personal and social education (PSE) programmes. In most schools, programmes for PSE have been improving. A growing strength is the increasing emphasis on a range of health education issues. However, approaches to learning and teaching are not always suited to achieving the aims of the programme. In addition, many schools still place insufficient emphasis on helping young people to be self-aware, to develop their values and beliefs, and to make informed choices and decisions.

3.3 Climate and support

Most secondary schools have a positive **climate for learning** and recognise that positive relationships and effective learning are likely to reduce the incidence of inappropriate behaviour. In a small number of schools where motivation is lacking, poor behaviour disrupts learning. Schools use a range of approaches to encourage positive behaviour, including well-judged reward systems. Some schools need to do more to engage all staff and pupils in establishing appropriate values for learning, such as mutual respect and teamwork. More detail on this aspect can be found in the HMIE report, *A Climate for Learning*.[15]

Bullying is an issue which schools take seriously. Almost all schools have clear approaches to dealing with bullying and pupils recognise this. Nevertheless, schools should continue to address bullying in a sensitive and proactive way.

Personal support for pupils remains a strong aspect of most secondary schools. Some schools have effectively improved collaboration among staff to meet the needs of all pupils through introducing new management structures and work practices in the delivery of personal support. Most schools are improving inter-agency working to help meet the needs of specific individuals and groups. Joint working is leading to more effective planning and is more effectively targeting support for individual pupils. Staff are beginning to use a range of strategies to monitor pupils' progress and make better use of this information to enable pupils to set appropriately challenging targets for their future performance. Arrangements to help pupils make decisions about course choices and future careers are effective in most schools. Further detail about the effectiveness of approaches to personal support can be found in a recent HMIE report.[16]

In most schools, **support for learning** is very good or good. Some key strengths are:

- good practice in primary/secondary transition focusing on specific individuals;
- a clear identification of pupils' needs and the setting of individualised targets;
- high-quality interactions between specialist staff and pupils in one-to-one work;

---

[15] *A Climate for Learning* (HMIE 2005)

[16] *Personal Support for Pupils in Scottish Schools* (HMIE 2004)

- an increasing focus on developing approaches to include more pupils in mainstream activities; and

- effective collaborative planning with a range of external agencies.

LEARNING SUPPORT

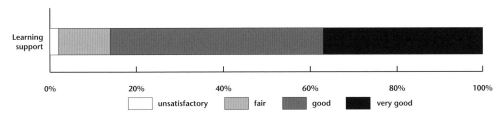

Distribution of quality indicator evaluations in the secondary sector, 2002-2005.

In around 15% of schools, support for learning has important weaknesses. Often in these cases, subject teachers have an insufficient understanding of the needs of pupils in their classes, or do not recognise fully the role learning support staff can play in their lessons. Teachers welcome pupils with a range of additional support needs into their classes, but challenges remain around integrating pupils who present behavioural difficulties. Many schools are using a range of effective approaches to meet the varied challenges which some pupils present. These often include flexible opportunities so that pupils can learn more productively including, if necessary, studying away from their usual classes on a temporary basis. There remains a need for schools and education authorities to provide further professional development in this area, including on developing effective teamwork amongst staff in providing for pupils with addtional support needs. Individualised educational programmes (IEPs) have become well established as key planning devices for helping to meet pupils' specific needs. Staff in some schools need to collaborate more effectively in creating and using appropriate long-term and short-term targets for pupils.

Not all schools have yet responded sufficiently to the *Race Relations Amendment Act (2004)*. The promotion of **equality** issues, including anti-racism and diversity, requires a greater emphasis in some schools, particularly through the curriculum.

Most schools have realised the importance of developing strong **partnerships with parents** to support their work. They enjoy purposeful relations with their School Boards and the majority encourage good levels of involvement of parents in the life of the school.

The Scottish Executive, local councils and other governing bodies have committed considerable resources to improving the **physical environment of schools** across the country. This includes both refurbishment and the construction of new buildings. The funding has made a considerable contribution to improving the environment for learners and staff. Improved learning environments have enriched pupils' learning experiences and increased their motivation. Despite the positive impact of the newly-built or refurbished schools, there are important or major weaknesses in some aspects of accommodation in almost half of the secondary schools inspected. Major issues include poor fabric, security of entrances, and poor accessibility for pupils and staff with disabilities.

4. Leadership and capacity to improve

4.1 Leadership

Leadership is very good or good in most schools.

LEADERSHIP

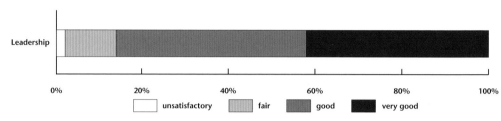

Distribution of quality indicator evaluations in the secondary sector, 2002-2005.

Senior managers in the most effective schools have a shared leadership culture which views improvement as the responsibility of all staff. Partnerships are built with a wide range of children's services to help meet the needs of all pupils. Staff, pupils, parents and other stakeholders have a shared vision for the future and a clear sense of direction. Leadership in these schools focuses clearly on improving pupils' learning experiences and the outcomes they achieve.

Headteachers, together with other members of the senior management team, usually fulfil a wide range of responsibilities effectively, including working with subject departments to evaluate and improve school performance. Senior managers usually support and guide these departments well. At times, however, some senior managers are too absorbed in day-to-day activities at the expense of upholding high expectations for learning and achievement. Together with principal teachers, they need to take a more active role in challenging subject departments to improve learning and teaching. Most principal teachers demonstrate relevant professional knowledge of their subject area or aspect. Many show strengths in curriculum development and administration.

Schools are going through a period of changes to management structures following *A Teaching Profession for the 21st Century*. It is too early to evaluate the full impact of the changes.

In a significant minority of schools, the quality of leadership has important or major weaknesses. This may result in important weaknesses in aspects of school ethos, poor teamwork, a lack of shared responsibility and accountability, and limited improvement in pupils' attainment and achievement.

4.2 Capacity to improve

Almost all schools have a range of approaches which help to identify strengths and areas for improvement, including the use of *How good is our school?*. Many schools also recognise the value of stakeholders' views and ideas and systematically seek and take account of them. The majority of schools plan appropriately for improvement and produce informative reports on standards and quality. In a number of cases, reports need to be more objective and evaluative and provide a clearer indication of the school's areas for improvement.

In around 45% of schools, self-evaluation for improvement has important weaknesses. Too often, schools and individual teachers lack a sense of ownership and shared responsibility for taking action to ensure improvement in learning, teaching and achievement. There is an insufficient focus on evaluating and improving the quality of learning and teaching and outcomes for pupils. Too little account is taken of pupils' and other stakeholders' views. In addition, the management of the self-evaluation system in many schools requires greater rigour and a more purposeful engagement of staff at all levels, in order to secure consistent improvement.

Overall, the secondary sector is seeking ways to become more effective in a rapidly changing environment. It has the capacity to take more responsibility for improvement and to be more accountable for the performance of all pupils. Secondary schools should now build on the strengths highlighted in this report to take on the challenging agenda of improving learning, raising achievement for all, and developing leadership at all levels.

Signpost to improvement in ‹‹
self-evaluation

- All staff take responsibility for improvement.
- Senior managers support and challenge departments in evaluating their performance, including the quality of learning and teaching.
- Staff, pupils and other stakeholders engage in evaluating quality.
- Staff have a self-evaluation focus on specific stages or aspects for improvement.
- Senior managers provide effective feedback to individuals.
- Staff create opportunities to discuss the findings of self-evaluation.
- Staff disseminate effective practice from within and outwith the school.
- Staff closely track pupils' progress.

Section Two: Special schools sector

1. Features and overview

1.1 The special schools sector

Special schools[17] provide education and, in the case of residential special schools, care and education for pupils whose needs cannot easily be met within mainstream schools. Some of the most vulnerable and challenging pupils in Scotland attend these schools.

Schools and free-standing units providing exclusively for pupils with additional support needs can have as many differences, one from another, as they have similarities. Depending on the area where the school is located, and the body which manages it, the school may only have pupils from primary stages, only pupils from secondary stages, or pupils from primary through to secondary. Some special schools also have nursery classes. Some schools provide care and education in residential settings[18] for pupils with a wide range of additional support needs. These are mainly, but not exclusively, independent schools. Some special schools have pupils with a wide range of educational needs. Others specialise. Some, for example, have pupils with severe and complex learning difficulties and others provide for pupils with social, emotional and behavioural difficulties. In addition, secure accommodation services in six locations provide care and education for pupils requiring secure arrangements.

The *Standards in Scotland's Schools etc (2000) Act* introduced the idea of 'the presumption of mainstreaming'. As a consequence, pupils should be educated in a mainstream school unless this is not suitable for the child, is not in the interests of other pupils, or incurs unreasonable expenditure. The percentage of pupils who are educated in special schools remains around one per cent of the total pupil population. The overall number of special schools also remains broadly constant. The recent *Additional Support for Learning Act (2004)* has developed the concept of 'special educational needs' into a wider view of 'additional support needs'. The result is that a larger number of children now can be described as having additional support needs than would have been described as having special educational needs.

The quality of the climate for learning, positive relationships and sense of teamwork among staff are very positive features of most special schools. Pastoral care and support for pupils are also very strong features in most schools. However, a number of special schools pay insufficient attention to ensuring that pupils achieve well across the curriculum and gain appropriate certification for their achievements. Some important issues in relation to leadership need also to be addressed.

---

[17] Throughout this report where the term 'special schools' is used it refers both to day special schools and to residential special schools. On occasion, the text indicates reference to only one type of special school. The word 'schools' includes those special units which are managed separately from the mainstream school within which they are located.

[18] See also: *Residential care and education: improving practice in residential special schools in Scotland* (Care Commission and HMIE 2005)

1.2 Key strengths

Key strengths of the special schools sector include the following:

- parents' satisfaction with almost all aspects of the work of the school;

- pupils' achievements in personal and social development;

- the commitment of teachers and support staff to pupils' care and education;

- the quality of pastoral care in most schools;

- the strength of partnerships with parents in most schools; and

- the positive climate for learning in most schools.

1.3 Aspects for improvement

This report identifies the following key themes as aspects for further improvement within special schools:

Leadership: Schools should improve their strategic leadership, including approaches to self-evaluation. Leadership should also focus on improving learning and teaching.

Learning and achievement: Pupils' learning experiences should be more effective, more motivating and cover a broader range of areas. The length of the school week should be the same as in mainstream schools to provide sufficient time for learning. Pupils should be encouraged to play a more active part in their own learning to improve their confidence and responsibility. They need to have more opportunities to work with and learn from each other. Their learning should be enlivened through more imaginative teaching, including the use of ICT. More use should be made of interesting homework tasks to encourage independent learning. Schools need to work more closely with parents to raise expectations and to help their children to learn at home.

Partnerships: Residential special schools and secure accommodation need to improve approaches to partnership working with authorities to ensure that the needs of pupils are fully considered.

Special schools 2

2. Key outcomes

Introduction

Within special schools, pupils' achievements and attainments are evaluated through their performance in the 5-14 curriculum and national qualifications (NQs) and through progress against targets which have been set within their individualised educational programmes (IEPs). It is appropriate to focus first on pupils' overall achievements before considering levels of attainment in this sector.

2.1 Broader achievements

Special schools commendably place a high priority on ensuring that pupils develop self-confidence and social competence. Pupils' achievements in aspects of personal and social development (PSD) are a clear strength of the special schools sector. Almost all pupils who attend special schools have individual targets for PSD. Residential special and day special schools provide a wide range of interesting and worthwhile opportunities to help pupils develop socially as confident individuals and to achieve in a variety of ways. Pupils successfully participate in enterprise activities, outdoor education and in a range of educational experiences based in their local communities. Most schools ensure that pupils experience success in communicating through the expressive arts by taking part in musical performances or creating and exhibiting art work.

Within residential special schools and day schools which provide solely for pupils with social, emotional and behavioural difficulties (SEBD), pupils' successes in PSD can be, in a number of cases, impressive. These schools help pupils overcome many barriers to their learning and some pupils make very positive progress relative to their starting points. Where schools have been successful, they have transformed vulnerable and challenging young people into young adults who are aware of the need to become responsible citizens. The young people welcome visitors to their school, and individually demonstrate respect for adults and peers. In the best cases, they are well prepared to re-integrate into mainstream school or move on successfully to further and occasionally higher education.

PERSONAL AND SOCIAL DEVELOPMENT

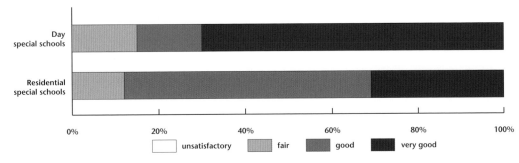

Distribution of quality indicator evaluations in the special schools sector, 2002-2005.

Although special schools are successful overall in helping pupils to become confident individuals and to contribute effectively, more still needs to be done to ensure that pupils also become successful learners and achieve well across the curriculum. Too many pupils within special schools are not achieving at high enough levels.

2.2 Attainment

Within those residential special and day special schools which make provision for pupils with more severe and complex learning difficulties, pupils generally achieve well in English language (or communication and language) and mathematics (or understanding and relating to the environment). Where there are well-planned experiences, pupils develop skills in listening and attending and they learn to respond and communicate in a variety of ways. This includes the use of signs and symbols and, for the small numbers of pupils who require this, through technological aids to communication. In the best examples, speech and language therapists work successfully in partnership with schools to develop whole-school communication strategies.

However, important weaknesses exist in pupils' attainment in English language in around a third of day special schools and in mathematics in more than a quarter of these schools. The picture is poorer still in residential special and day special schools which provide exclusively for pupils with SEBD. Important weaknesses are present in pupils' attainment in English language and in mathematics in most of these schools.

Weaknesses in attainment can be attributed, in part, to a number of factors.

- The length of the school week for pupils in around half of day special schools, particularly those which make provision solely for pupils with SEBD, is shorter than in mainstream schools.

- Pupils attending schools catering for pupils with SEBD often experience major interruptions to their learning before being placed there.

- Some schools, particularly those for pupils with SEBD and residential special schools, experience difficulty in attracting or retaining teachers with qualifications in a subject specialism. This affects pupils' attainments in key areas of the curriculum.

- On occasions, pupils' behavioural difficulties mask undiagnosed learning difficulties, particularly related to literacy skills.

2.3 Stakeholders' views

- **Pupils:** Most pupils enjoyed being in school. They felt that their school was generally good at dealing with bullying and they knew who to speak to if they were unhappy at school. In a few schools which catered for pupils with SEBD and in some residential special schools, a number of pupils felt that the behaviour of a few pupils could be improved. Also in these schools, a number of pupils felt that they did not get the right amount of homework, nor did teachers always check their homework regularly.

- **Teachers and staff:** Teachers and support staff enjoyed working in special schools. In most schools, they felt that there was mutual respect among staff and between staff and pupils. In some schools, staff felt that they would like to be more fully involved in decision making.

- **Parents:** Parents were happy with the services provided in most special schools and thought that their children were better served than in a mainstream school. They also felt that schools involved them well in reviewing their child's progress. Some parents wanted to know more about how they could support their child with homework or home-learning activities. In a number of schools, parents expressed concerns about the school buildings.

- **Authorities placing pupils in residential special schools and secure accommodation:** Those authorities which responded frequently praised the positive relationships staff had with young people. Some authorities commented positively on the improved achievements of pupils.

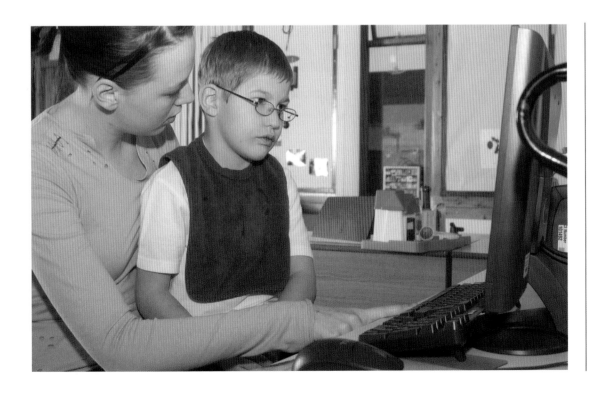

3. Meeting the needs of all learners

3.1 Learning and teaching

>> **Signpost to improvement in learning and teaching**

Staff:

- have appropriately high expectations for all their pupils;
- ensure that individual learning targets are always challenging and effectively blended with broader curricular planning;
- provide opportunities for effective home learning;
- share the criteria for success with pupils and consistently provide them with feedback on their learning;
- foster and develop pupils' abilities to engage collaboratively with each other; and
- develop pupils' skills of independent working.

The commitment of teachers is a strength in special schools. For the most part, teachers create positive learning environments to help pupils to learn. They use praise well to build pupils' self-confidence and encourage achievement. Most teachers have good relationships with their pupils and have a clear understanding of their individual needs and learning difficulties. Teachers use good quality direct teaching with individuals and groups and provide pupils with clear instructions, directions and explanations. Increasingly, they give pupils feedback about their learning to help them improve. Most teachers show patience and understanding when working with pupils with significant difficulties. Most create learning environments which successfully motivate and interest pupils. However, the quality of teaching is often too variable within schools and good practice is not always consistently shared or built upon. Special schools do not always make sufficiently good use of homework, or work with parents to develop home-learning opportunities.

Within the context of committed teachers and overall good quality of learning experiences, improvements are still needed in meeting the learning needs of all pupils. Too often learning is teacher-directed with pupils being passive recipients. Learning experiences are frequently not organised in ways which easily encourage pupils to learn by doing and by interacting with and learning from each other. The use of ICT to enhance pupils' learning experiences needs to be developed further. Enriching experiences using technology such as digital cameras, video recording, interactive whiteboards and switches are too limited. In the 14% of schools where the overall quality of pupils' learning experiences is evaluated as very good, pupils experience learning in a wide range of contexts, including opportunities to learn collaboratively and alongside pupils in mainstream schools.

THE TEACHING PROCESS/PUPILS' LEARNING EXPERIENCES

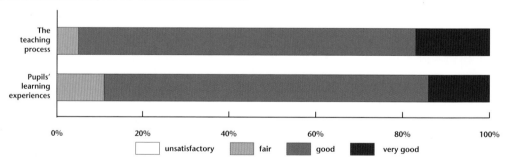

Distribution of quality indicator evaluations in day special schools, 2002-2005.

Special schools 2

Generally, special schools need to have higher expectations of pupils' achievements. In particular, over half of the schools which provide solely for pupils with SEBD need to be better at identifying their pupils' different learning needs. Too often, these schools concentrate on how pupils 'present' behavioural difficulties, without effectively seeking out and addressing the reasons for these difficulties.

3.2 Curriculum

Overall, the majority of special schools provide a good curriculum. They make use of national 5-14 guidelines, guidelines for the elaborated 5-14 curriculum and NQs, particularly at Access levels, when planning their curriculum. Many schools use some degree of curriculum flexibility to ensure that they meet pupils' diverse learning needs and enable all pupils to achieve appropriately. A number of schools make use of college courses to provide increased learning opportunities. However, there is room for special schools to improve the quality of the curriculum which they provide. Special schools need to take action to monitor the arrangements for flexibility which they have put in place. They also need to ensure that wherever possible they provide pupils with opportunities to have their achievements recognised through certification.

STRUCTURE OF THE CURRICULUM

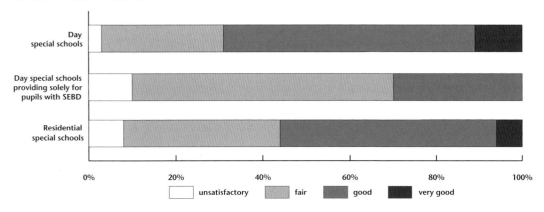

Distribution of quality indicator evaluations in the special schools sector, 2002-2005.

The need to improve the curriculum remains a particular issue for special schools which provide solely for pupils with SEBD. It is difficult for schools to develop pupils as successful learners when, in the majority of cases, the short length of the school week remains an issue which needs to be resolved. A number of special schools have experienced tensions between ensuring a broad, balanced and holistic experience for all and providing for individual learning needs. Historically, IEPs were introduced as a means of meeting the learning needs and personalising the curriculum for pupils with special educational needs. Almost all special schools make use of IEPs. Commonly, schools set targets in IEPs in English (or communication and language), mathematics (or understanding and relating to the environment), and PSD. These are often, but not always, drawn up in consultation with pupils, parents and partner agencies.

Signpost to improvement in ‹‹
the curriculum

- *Pupils have broad curricular experiences underpinned by opportunities to have their attainment and achievement appropriately accredited.*
- *Staff ensure that any curriculum flexibility arrangement is carefully planned to meet pupils' needs and includes appropriate opportunities to certificate pupils' broader achievements.*
- *Pupils' individual targets are effectively blended with broader curricular planning to ensure that outcomes for pupils are set within a clear and appropriate context.*
- *The length of the school week matches that of mainstream schools.*
- *Lunchtimes and breaks are used effectively to provide time for planned learning activities to be undertaken. This is particularly important in those schools which make provision for pupils with complex and multiple learning difficulties.*

>> **Signpost to improvement in IEPs:**

They:

- *are drawn up in consultation with pupils, parents and appropriate agencies;*
- *have clearly stated long-term targets which cover a school year;*
- *have appropriate short-term targets which are 'steps towards' each long-term target;*
- *indicate the measures of success for each long-term and short-term target and the means by which the target will be achieved; and*
- *are, wherever possible, stated in terms of curricular targets which a pupil has to achieve.*

Although IEPs are widely used in special schools, their quality is variable. Often IEPs complicate, rather than simplify, the process of meeting pupils' learning needs. In some cases, targets can be insufficiently challenging. In others, pupils' progress towards achieving their targets is not monitored or tracked with sufficient clarity to promote learning and progression. Over-elaborate IEPs can work against staff, pupils, and parents having a clear understanding of the intended learning outcomes. In a few schools, the use of IEPs has resulted in the development of fragmented learning experiences for pupils. Schools need to ensure that 'priority learning targets' are set for individual pupils in the context of a well-designed curriculum which encompasses a wide variety of different learning experiences.

3.3 Climate and support

Despite the challenges which arise from the diverse and wide-ranging needs of their pupils, almost all special schools successfully create a positive **climate for learning**. In most schools, very good relationships exist among staff, including care and education staff and between staff and pupils. Although pupils sometimes display extremely challenging behaviour, either as a result of their disabilities, because of learning difficulties or through social and emotional factors, a number of schools successfully promote good behaviour and have a strong sense of equality and fairness.

CLIMATE AND RELATIONSHIPS

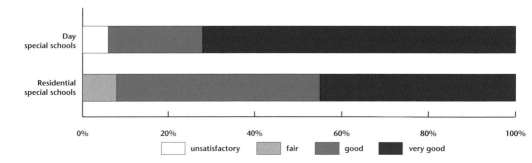

Distribution of quality indicator evaluations in the special schools sector, 2002-2005.

An overall strength of day special schools is the importance which staff place on providing pupils with strong **personal support** and **pastoral care**. In most special schools pastoral care is very good and staff pay very good attention to meeting pupils' individual care needs, to matters of health and safety and to child protection. In a small number of schools there remains a need to ensure that all staff are trained in child protection procedures. Appropriately, all pupils in special schools have targets for personal and social development within their IEPs. In some residential special schools the links between pupils' PSD targets and their Care Plans should be made more explicit.

PASTORAL CARE

Day special schools

| 0% | 20% | 40% | 60% | 80% | 100% |

☐ unsatisfactory ▨ fair ▨ good ■ very good

Distribution of quality indicator evaluations in day special schools, 2002-2005.

Within the context of strong support for individual pupils, some schools which provide solely for pupils with SEBD need to continue to improve their approaches to personal support. Similarly, over a third of residential special schools need to improve some aspects of their arrangements for the care and welfare of young people. This includes the need to improve their approaches to risk management, security in accommodation and arrangements in respect of child protection.

Special schools should give a high priority to the all-round development of children and young people and continue to put an appropriately strong emphasis on personal support and care and welfare. As the behaviour of young people becomes more challenging, schools need to pay greater attention to their methods of supporting these vulnerable children while also ensuring staff are safe. In best practice, there is a highly structured but safe climate in which young people know the boundaries. Within such an environment, restraint can be used safely and appropriately by care and education staff who have been provided with sensitive and regular training.

Almost all education authority special schools have strong and effective links with parents. Common strengths include regular communications between parents and teachers, often using a simple but effective daily diary system. **Partnerships** are a positive feature of almost all special schools. For example, in the majority of residential special schools, staff work closely with a range of therapists to ensure pupils' physical and sensory needs are well met. In these schools, key workers from care and education backgrounds work closely together to support young people to develop their competences in learning and social skills. Staff in day special schools also work well with a range of other professionals including educational psychologists and speech and language therapists to meet pupils' learning and social needs.

Signpost to improvement in ‹‹ care and welfare in residential special schools

- *There are regular health and safety checks of accommodation and facilities and high standards in fire safety and school security are established.*
- *Accommodation and facilities promote independence, privacy and dignity for pupils.*
- *Staff carry out broad and specific risk assessment to ensure pupils' care and welfare.*
- *A range of training which highlights the values of the school and ensures consistent, fair and firm responses to challenging situations is provided for care and education staff.*
- *Policies on no smoking and safe use of the internet are vigilantly promoted.*

Integrated working in residential special schools involving key care workers and key teachers provides an 'educationally rich' environment by supporting pupils to complete school work. It also promotes interest in learning through, for example, encouraging educational visits in the evenings and at weekends.

During recent years, many independent residential special schools have made considerable financial investment in their buildings, resulting in much improved **accommodation and facilities**. These schools generally have good strategic plans for continuous improvement of accommodation, which ensure future development or refurbishment. They take account of health and safety requirements arising from national care standards and disability legislation. In addition, a number of local authorities have developed clear strategic plans to improve their special school estates. These include schools being rebuilt and refurbished often to high specifications.

However, despite improvements in some schools, important weaknesses in the environment for learning continue to exist in over a quarter of special schools. Weaknesses include the decaying fabric of buildings and classrooms and facilities no longer meeting the needs of all pupils who attend the schools. A number of special schools are found in generally inappropriate locations for education in the 21st century. For example, some schools for pupils with severe and complex learning difficulties were originally built within hospital grounds at a distance from residential areas.

ACCOMMODATION AND FACILITIES

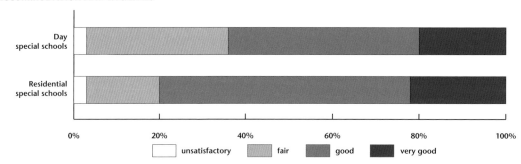

Distribution of quality indicator evaluations in the special schools sector, 2002-2005.

Special schools 2

4. Leadership and capacity to improve

4.1 Leadership

The number of special schools where leadership was very good has increased. In these schools, there is a greater focus on improving the quality of pupils' learning experiences and an increasing emphasis on evaluating the work of the school with a view to improving learning. However, leadership in almost one in three schools has important weaknesses.

LEADERSHIP

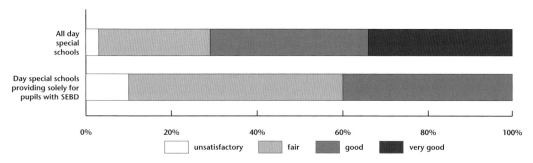

Distribution of quality indicator evaluations in day special schools, 2002-2005.

Signpost to improvement in ‹‹ leadership (1)

Leaders:

- *have a key focus on developing learning and teaching to improve outcomes for pupils;*
- *ensure that they have a strong visible presence in school;*
- *maintain the respect of staff, pupils and parents and carers;*
- *develop good communication among staff;*
- *have a very good knowledge of individual pupils;*
- *have clearly defined responsibilities in relation to quality improvement; and*
- *in residential special schools, strengthen links with other similar establishments and with local authorities so that good practice can be shared appropriately.*

Headteachers and promoted staff within special schools are, generally, professionally competent and committed to their schools. Most are well qualified and have gained additional qualifications relevant to the needs of the pupils within their schools. They have personal credibility with staff, pupils and parents. They effectively manage staff teams, which in many cases consist of both teachers and large numbers of support staff. Headteachers in special schools also work effectively with a number of external agencies and co-ordinate the work of these agencies for the benefit of pupils.

Important weaknesses in leadership continue to exist within certain types of special school. In particular, the quality of leadership needs to improve in more than half of day special schools which make provision solely for pupils with SEBD. In these schools, and others, headteachers need to monitor and evaluate more effectively the work of the school and provide a clearer focus on improving the quality of pupils' learning experiences and achievements within a suitably broad curriculum.

The nature and complexity of special schools make it essential for headteachers to provide clear direction and leadership to support and challenge staff and pupils consistently and visibly. In order to build capacity for improvement within special schools and to plan for the future, education authorities and senior managers should provide opportunities for leadership development.

>> **Signpost to improvement in leadership (2)**

Local authorities can provide leadership for special schools through:

- *ensuring that they have a local strategic plan to address the wide range of additional support needs which exist within their local area;*
- *clarifying the role that residential special schools play in meeting the needs of pupils for whose education the local authority is responsible;*
- *satisfying themselves about the quality of provision which is offered in their own special schools and in residential special schools within which they place pupils;*
- *providing an appropriate level of partnership working with these schools and offering support where that is appropriate; and*
- *ensuring that the fabric, condition and location of special school buildings provide an appropriate and motivating environment for learning.*

Improving the leadership of special schools is also important at local authority level. Local authorities need to have a clear strategic overview of how they will meet the wide range of additional support needs for which they have responsibility.

4.2 Capacity to improve

In the majority of special schools, the process of planning for improvement has become well established. Special schools make good use of a range of approaches including questionnaires to stakeholders and *How good is our school?* to identify areas for improvement. In schools where approaches to improvement are having a positive impact on pupils' learning experiences, there are clear procedures to track pupils' progress, to monitor and evaluate classroom practice and to involve teachers in peer and self-evaluation. However, in most schools there is scope for improvement in this area. Too often teachers and support staff are not sufficiently involved in identifying priorities for improvement and are not sufficiently reflective in their practice.

Half of the special schools inspected between 2002 and 2005 had weaknesses in self-evaluation. In these schools, there was no established culture of self-evaluation for improvement. Where self-evaluation was undertaken, it often consisted of no more than routine monitoring by senior managers without a clear focus on improving learning and teaching. Self-evaluation was rarely embraced by all members of staff.

SELF-EVALUATION/PLANNING FOR IMPROVEMENT

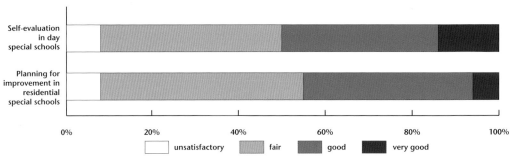

Distribution of quality indicator evaluations in the special schools sector, 2002-2005.

Special schools 2

Self-evaluation for improvement remains a significant weakness in residential special schools. In these schools, managers need to work with staff directly in classrooms and in care settings and involve them in discussions about improvements to learning, teaching and care through reflecting on existing practice. In residential special schools and secure accommodation services, few schools effectively use national care standards and quality indicators to evaluate their work and identify priorities for improvement. Very few residential special schools have undertaken strategic planning in relation to the development and improvement of educational practice and care.

Throughout the special school sector, there needs to be a clearer emphasis on evaluating practice with a view to improving learning experiences and meeting individual pupils' needs.

This report highlights areas of strength and the directions which special schools should take in order to improve the quality of the curriculum and pupils' learning experiences. Building on its current strengths, the special schools sector has the capacity to improve and to meet these challenges.

Signpost to improvement in «« self-evaluation and impact

All staff:

- *are involved in reflecting on the aims, purpose and values of their own school;*
- *have a shared understanding of their role in providing a high-quality service which focuses on meeting pupils' learning needs; and*
- *effectively use tools such as quality indicators, national care standards and evidence gathered through monitoring to evaluate strengths and weaknesses, identify priorities and stimulate focused improvement.*

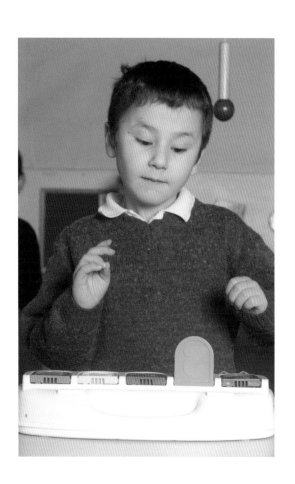

Section Two: College sector

1. Features and overview

1.1 The college sector

Scotland's colleges provide learners with opportunities to develop personal skills and skills for employment, enabling them to contribute to the economy and the wider social and cultural environment and to enhance their own quality of life. They have motivated a wide cross-section of our society to become lifelong learners.

Colleges operate in widely varying social, economic and geographical environments. They have adopted a responsive and flexible approach in expanding and broadening provision to satisfy the demands of employers and communities in continually changing economic and social circumstances, and to meet the needs of learners from a range of backgrounds. The sector has expanded to the extent that in 2005 almost one in ten Scots participated in activities offered by Scotland's colleges. Some colleges serve scattered and diverse rural populations. Others operate from urban locations, with most learners coming from within a relatively small area. Most colleges offer a broad curriculum but a number specialise in particular subject areas and draw learners from across Scotland and beyond. Recent consolidation in the sector has had the effect of reducing the overall number of colleges from 46 to 43.

Students access college learning through community-based centres, work places, distance learning, and online packages as well as in the more traditional settings of classrooms, workshops and laboratories on a main campus. A number of colleges have new, modern accommodation. Others operating from older buildings on well-established campuses have plans at advanced stages of development to improve their learning and teaching accommodation.

Colleges are funded by the Scottish Further and Higher Education Funding Council (SFC) and also gain other income through contracts with employers and other agencies, for example to carry out government-funded training. Some colleges, in particular those which are partners in the University of the Highlands and Islands Millennium Institute, offer a range of degree programmes and research opportunities for learners.

Details on HMIE findings in the college sector are available in annual reports[19] published by HMIE to provide an analysis of the findings of that year's reviews, and an overview[20] of findings across all years of the review cycle to date.

[19] Analysis of HMIE Reviews of Standards and Quality in Further Education, academic year 2003-04
[20] HMIE reviews of Standards and Quality in Further Education, an overview, academic years 2000-01 to 2003-04

ING SCOTTISH EDUCATION_SECTOR REPORTS

1.2 Key strengths

Key strengths of the college sector include the following.

- Colleges have delivered a range of programmes and learning opportunities tailored to meet the needs of employers, local communities and the individual.

- Close links between colleges and a range of partners, including schools, higher education institutions (HEIs), community groups, employers and the enterprise networks have created effective learning opportunities and progression routes for learners from a range of backgrounds.

- Colleges have been successful in encouraging lifelong learning through a wide range of flexible arrangements which have led to learners achieving well and developing core skills, personal skills, vocational skills and other skills for employability.

- Effective educational leadership has ensured that colleges have focused on delivering inclusive learning strategies. This has been supported by effective arrangements to ensure that learners from diverse backgrounds receive appropriate guidance and support to help them progress to employment opportunities or further study.

1.3 Aspects for improvement

This report identifies the following key themes as aspects for further improvement in the college sector.

Self-evaluation and its impact

- Colleges should continue to develop and implement rigorously systematic self-evaluation procedures, with the particular aims of improving retention and achievement.

- Better use should be made of programme and unit attainment data to evaluate the effectiveness of programme delivery.

- Self-evaluation procedures, taking enhanced account of learner views, should focus more on evaluating and improving the quality of learning and teaching.

Sharing of good practice

- Colleges should do more to identify, capture and use effectively the good practice which exists in many aspects of their provision and use it to enhance the quality of less effective aspects.

Learning and teaching

- Colleges should ensure that there is sufficient staff expertise, access to equipment and facilities, and variety in teaching approaches to ensure the effective contribution of ICT to the learning process.

2. Key outcomes

Introduction

The Scottish Executive's five-year strategy for lifelong learning, *Life through Learning: Learning through Life* (Scottish Executive, 2003), recognises the important role that Scotland's colleges play in driving change in Scotland's society and the Scottish economy, in developing in learners the range of skills they require to participate fully as citizens in society, and in preparing learners for their role in supporting economic development in Scotland. In recent years, Scotland's colleges have increased numbers of learners in the sector and implemented a range of flexible strategies which have supported learners in their lifelong learning.

2.1 Learner outcomes

Typically, colleges provide **education and training** from level 1 to level 8 in the Scottish Credit and Qualifications Framework (SCQF). Some offer programmes of study at higher levels, usually in conjunction with a partner HEI. In colleges, formal attainment is accredited by various awarding bodies, but predominantly through the Scottish Qualifications Authority (SQA). The SFC publishes annually an analysis of learner attainment from returns made by colleges on retention rates, and unit and programme attainment rates.[21]

A key area of economic development in which colleges play an important role is in supporting **workforce development**. One way in which colleges contribute to this is through the delivery of Scottish Vocational Qualifications (SVQ) programmes to Skillseekers, Modern Apprentices and others in a broad range of subjects.

Most learners in Scotland's colleges have a positive learning experience and achieve and progress well. In practical subjects, learners often develop vocational skills at levels above the minimum required. In part-time further education (FE) and higher education (HE) programmes most learners complete the programme and attain the relevant named award. As well as attaining formal qualifications, learners develop further their core skills, personal skills, vocational skills and other skills for employability during their time in a college.

However, attendance, retention and completion rates are still poor in many programmes. In some cases, learners either withdraw from their programme early or attend classes infrequently or irregularly. This often contributes to low programme attainment.

---

[21] *Student and staff performance indicators for further education colleges in Scotland 2003-04,* available at **http://www.sfc.ac.uk**

A minority of learners do not develop their core skills well, sometimes because of insufficient contextualisation, coverage or integration within programmes. Where this occurs, it often contributes to low participation in lessons and associated poor attainment. In more than a few cases learners' literacy and numeracy skills are developed reactively rather than as part of a programme of systematic and sustained development of skills.[22] Over the last four years of review, evaluations show that there is still considerable room for improvement in providing learners with the best possible opportunities to learn and to achieve. The SFC is promoting a quality enhancement theme on **learner retention and achievement** to encourage colleges to adopt measures which will improve these aspects.

STUDENT ACHIEVEMENT

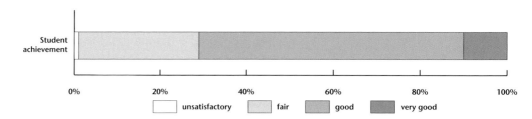

Distribution of quality indicator evaluations in college sector subject reviews, 2000-2004.

2.2 The views of learners

An analysis of the views of learners[23] identified several factors which learners consider to be influential to their overall progress and achievement. These factors include the quality of teaching and approachability of teaching staff, ethos and group dynamics, the design and organisational aspects of programmes, the availability of appropriate guidance, induction and support, and the extent of the match between learning preferences of learners and teaching approaches. In respect of all these factors, learners in Scotland's colleges have consistently expressed favourable views on their experiences, with staff commitment and effective support seen as particularly strong features of college life.

3. Meeting the needs of all learners

3.1 Learning and teaching

Within most college environments, the use of a wide range of stimulating learning and teaching approaches fosters and maintains the interest of learners. Most teaching staff take appropriate account of learners' prior learning and experience in adapting the pace and level of learning to meet learner needs. Staff help learners, including mature students and adult returners, to improve self-confidence and skills for employability. In most cases, staff also challenge learners to achieve beyond the minimum level required for completion of their programme.

---

[22] *Changing Lives: Adult Literacy and Numeracy in Scotland. A report by HMIE* (2005)

[23] *Student Learning in Scottish Further Education Colleges. A report for SFEFC by HMIE* (2004)

Over the four-year review cycle ending in 2004, much sector-leading and innovative practice was identified to support improvements in further education. A selection of these examples reflecting learning and teaching practice worthy of dissemination, may be explored on the HMIE website.

However, teaching staff occasionally adopt minimalist approaches such as teaching almost exclusively to assessment demands. Where excessive or inappropriate assessment practices are applied, these often serve to obstruct rather than aid learning. They also burden students and demotivate staff. In a few cases, learners are not fully engaged in the learning process and teaching staff do not take the opportunity to deploy an appropriate range of teaching methods. In a few cases, imaginative use of ICT has enhanced the learning process. However, limitations in staff familiarity and expertise, insufficiently varied approaches to the use of ICT and occasionally limited access to ICT adversely affect learning experiences.

TEACHING AND LEARNING PROCESS

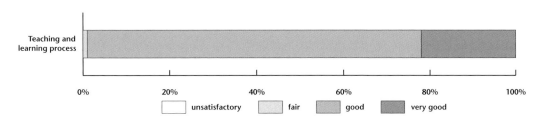

Distribution of quality indicator evaluations in college sector subject reviews, 2000-2004.

In most subjects, learners benefit from engagement with well-qualified staff who have up-to-date professional expertise, supported by effective continuing professional development. In most subjects, staff provide effective guidance and support for learning. However, in a few cases, ineffective career review and continuous professional development leave subject staff poorly equipped to provide learners with the help and support they need for a relevant, rich and rewarding learning experience.

Signpost to improvement in ‹‹
learning and teaching

- *Reflecting on their own preferred learning approaches helps learners develop their learning skills.*
- *Learning experiences help learners develop core skills as well as skills specific to their programmes.*
- *Staff consciously help learners develop the personal, academic and vocational skills necessary for citizenship and employability.*
- *Learning contexts promote the effective use of modern technology to enhance the learning experience.*
- *Staff use formative and summative assessment to help learners gauge the progress they have made, and encourage them to extend their learning.*

3.2 Programmes

All colleges offer flexible programmes in a range of subject disciplines. Many colleges promote a broad range of flexible learning opportunities in various locations. The delivery of programmes at times and in locations convenient to learners encourages a wide range of participants to enrol and complete programmes of study. Almost all colleges offer distance-learning programmes and are developing an increasing range of online learning materials. In a few colleges, the range of programmes offered on a flexible basis is narrow and does not offer sufficient learner choice. Many staff in colleges use strong links with external agencies to incorporate work-based experiences, fieldwork and project work within curriculum delivery. Many colleges deliver programmes in adult literacy and numeracy and pre-vocational skills through effective **partnership working** with local authority departments and community agencies. Links with community learning and with social work are particularly strong in a number of colleges, and facilitate education in the community for disadvantaged groups of learners. Links which colleges have established with schools provide pupils with learning experiences which are not available in school contexts. Practical difficulties including transport and the problems of aligning timetables among several schools and their local college occasionally create barriers to effective collaboration between schools and colleges. Partnerships between colleges and HEIs provide learners with clear and often well-integrated progression pathways to degrees.

3.3 Access and inclusion; guidance and support

Collaborative activities with a wide range of partners have encouraged stronger participation rates leading to enhanced work-based learning opportunities and improved progression routes for learners. Improved guidance and support arrangements have contributed to learners having positive learning experiences overall and have helped develop their skills for lifelong learning.

Colleges have played an important role in improving **access and inclusion** for a broad range of learners. Strong teamworking, partnership, shared commitment to success, good rapport and mutual respect all contribute to the quality of access and inclusion. Student enrolments in colleges increased by around 20% between 1995 and 2000. Since 2001, fundable activity within the sector has not increased significantly, and there has been a small decline in individual enrolments.

ACCESS AND INCLUSION

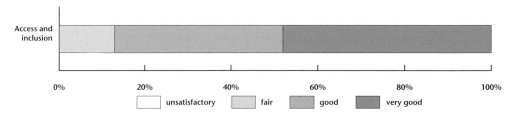

Distribution of quality indicator evaluations in college sector college reviews, 2000-2004.

In recent years, colleges have invested heavily in expanding and developing their **guidance and support services** to help learners. These overarching services have become increasingly accessible to all learners at all points in their learning experience. They have provided induction and pre-entry screening arrangements, referral systems for staff and learners, and ongoing monitoring of learner progress. In a few instances, guidance and support arrangements in colleges have not supported the early intervention necessary to sustain learner retention and achievement.

3.4 Resources

Recent improvements in college **accommodation** and investment in up-to-date equipment and materials have provided learners with stimulating learning environments and essential modern facilities. In most instances, the classroom and workshop ethos is positive and the atmosphere in which students learn is friendly, relaxed, informal yet purposeful, and conducive to learning. In a few cases, poor or insufficient accommodation and outdated or inadequate equipment provide a serious disincentive to learners and have contributed to poor retention and attainment rates.

4. Leadership and capacity to improve

4.1 Leadership

In most colleges, effective educational leadership and good communication keep staff throughout the organisation well informed about key priorities, aims and objectives.

Appropriate mission, vision and value statements, often placing the learner at the centre, are usually well understood by staff. In most colleges, productive partnerships are in place between college staff and employers, community organisations and other educational institutions such as universities and schools. Partnerships at strategic and operational level inform managers about stakeholder needs. Other partnerships with employers and community groups support the learning process and help to develop learners' skills for employability and citizenship.

EDUCATIONAL LEADERSHIP AND DIRECTION

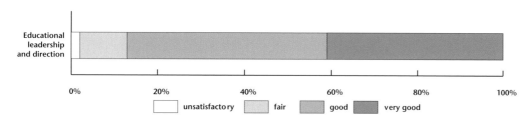

Distribution of quality indicator evaluations in college sector college reviews, 2000-2004.

At the operational level, a range of posts and responsibilities ensure the implementation of plans for the delivery of the curriculum in a range of modes. In most colleges, the planning process is well established and comprehensive, with clearly defined strategic priorities and operational targets. Generally, operational plans relate well to colleges' strategic aims. However, target setting is often insufficiently specific, and milestones and responsibilities are not clearly identified, limiting opportunities for colleges to implement effective action planning to bring about improvement.

4.2 Capacity to improve

In most colleges, quality assurance and improvement arrangements have developed and become more comprehensive over the past four years. Where programme teams have implemented rigorous and well-informed self-evaluation processes, this has often led to improvements in the learner experience. Similarly, where programme teams evaluate learning and teaching and share good practice in teaching approaches, this often leads to individual staff adopting more effective methods.

Most colleges collect evidence from learners, employers and other stakeholders in order to evaluate the level of client satisfaction. More than a few colleges also recognise the important contribution that non-teaching functions make to the learner experience and have extended self-evaluation and improvement processes to all areas impacting on learning and teaching.

A number of specific benefits have accrued from self-evaluation and improvement activity including:

- improved retention rates, leading to improved attainment in some subjects;
- improvements in learning and teaching approaches; and
- better use of access to ICT to develop self-confidence or independence in learning.

However, despite developments in quality improvement arrangements over the last few years, weaknesses are still prevalent in the approaches of some programme teams and colleges to quality assurance and improvement activities.

College 2

Reviewers find that programme teams often:

- make insufficient use of programme and unit attainment data in the analysis and evaluation of the effectiveness of programme delivery;

- fail to identify or grasp responsibilities for assuring and improving the quality of the learner experience; and

- do not apply self-evaluation and improvement activity systematically to learning and teaching.

QUALITY ASSURANCE AND IMPROVEMENT

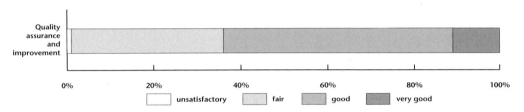

Distribution of quality indicator evaluations in college sector subject reviews, 2000-2004.

Weaknesses at college level in quality improvement often relate to:

- insufficient or ineffective ways to identify, capture and use effectively good practice in some areas of activity to help address weaknesses in other key areas;

- failure to extend the arrangements for quality assurance to all areas of the college with an impact on the learner; and

- failure to monitor whether planned actions are implemented and whether they are effective.

QUALITY IMPROVEMENT

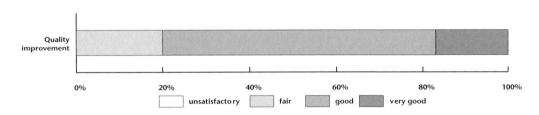

Distribution of quality indicator evaluations in college sector college reviews, 2000-2004.

In recent years most colleges have demonstrated increased maturity in developing and implementing systems and procedures to help deliver effective learning experiences for a wide and expanding range of learners, and to meet the needs of society and the economy. Overall, colleges are well placed to build on current strengths and enhance further the experiences of learners.

Signpost to improvement in ‹‹
quality assurance and
improvement

- *Staff at all levels accept their responsibilities for assuring and improving the quality of the learner experience, and take full ownership of self-evaluation and improvement activities.*

- *Staff use attainment data at unit and programme level to inform planning for improvement activities.*

- *Staff review the levels and range of programmes delivered in order to meet better the needs of learners and employers.*

- *Programme teams evaluate teaching and learning systematically with a view to improving the learning process.*

- *Colleges ensure that plans at all levels include appropriate targets for improvement on which progress is monitored rigorously.*

- *Colleges set in place structured arrangements for identifying, capturing and disseminating good practice and securing its adoption.*

- *Colleges extend their arrangements for quality assurance and improvement beyond curricular areas to all support and other areas which have an impact on the learner.*

Section Two: Community learning and development

1. Features and overview

1.1 The community learning and development sector

Community learning and development (CLD) refers to informal learning and social development work with individuals and groups within their communities. This diverse sector comprises three main educational activities:

- youth work;

- adult learning in the community (including adult classes, literacy and numeracy, parenting education and family learning); and

- building community capacity.

In communities throughout Scotland, local authorities and partner agencies in the public and voluntary sectors provide a diverse range of mainly informal learning opportunities for young people and adults. They also support community organisations to improve their communities and, where appropriate, to deliver local services. CLD provision is delivered in widely varying social, economic and geographical environments and in a wide range of community settings. Participation in CLD activities is voluntary. Learning programmes are developed through negotiation and dialogue between staff and participants in CLD programmes.

During the period covered by this report, strategic and operational management arrangements for the CLD sector have been changing as a result of a significant amount of legislation and guidance. Activities included:

- developing partnership arrangements between providers to improve the co-ordination and delivery of local services;

- contributing to the delivery of the community regeneration statement *Better communities in Scotland: closing the gap*;

- delivering, with further education colleges, a new programme to improve levels of adult literacy and numeracy in Scotland;

- contributing to the community engagement aspect of Community Planning as set out in the *Local Government in Scotland Act 2003*;

- developing local strategies for community learning and development based on three national priorities set out in the guidance *Working and Learning Together to Build Stronger Communities*;

- developing approaches to self-evaluation based on *How good is our community learning and development?*; and

- responding to the lifelong learning strategy for Scotland *Life Through Learning: Learning Through Life.*

Local authorities across Scotland adopt different service structures within which to locate their CLD services. These arrangements influence the priority given to aspects of CLD. As a result, the strength of the CLD contribution to wider initiatives such as integrated community schools, learning communities, early years initiatives, community regeneration, community safety and cultural, sports and arts developments varies from council to council.

The sector is slowly developing the professional self-confidence and infrastructure to emphasise and publicise the difference that CLD services make to participants, particularly those from disadvantaged groups. It is also beginning to develop more effective approaches to self-evaluation and improvement. Strategic and operational planning for CLD is very effective in a few local authorities but much less so in around half. Overall, the CLD sector is particularly well developed in its partnership work with a range of other services, agencies and community and voluntary organisations. There remains a challenge for the sector to gather and use performance information to evaluate provision systematically and to improve services.

Further details about the quality of CLD provision are available in the HMIE report summarising the findings of the cycle of CLD inspections across all local authorities (forthcoming).

1.2 Key strengths

Overall, the key strengths in the CLD sector include:

- examples of innovative and effective work with disadvantaged individuals and groups;

- the overall quality of youth work and adult learning provision;

- the overall achievements of young people, adults and communities supported by CLD provision;

- the commitment of staff to the values of CLD work and their motivational and relationship skills;

- effective partnership work with a wide range of agencies in almost all local authorities; and

- effective operational leadership for CLD in most local authorities.

Community learning and development 2

1.3 Aspects for improvement

This report identifies the following key themes as aspects for further improvement in the sector.

Assessment:

- the use of assessment processes to ensure that young people can identify and build on their learning and development through youth work

Self-evaluation and planning:

- the use and impact of self-evaluation for quality improvement in a majority of local authorities

- the effectiveness of processes to evaluate the impact of community capacity building work

- the quality of strategic, operational and improvement planning in about half of the local authorities

Staffing and accommodation:

- the effectiveness with which staff are deployed and provision for their continuing training and development in about half of the local authorities

- the quality and appropriateness of accommodation and facilities for CLD work

2. Key outcomes

Introduction

During the period covered by this report, national priorities for CLD were introduced by the Scottish Executive. They relate to achievement through learning for adults, achievement through learning for young people and achievement through building community capacity.

In many local authorities, CLD inspections focused on geographical areas with high levels of multiple deprivation as measured by the Scottish Index of Multiple Deprivation[24] (SIMD) 2004. Many of the communities inspected were in urban areas and areas formerly characterised by mining, steel, fishing and textile industries. In the majority of CLD inspections, the levels of unemployment were significantly above the national average in the years 2002-2005.

The achievements of adults and young people outlined below increased the capacity of local communities to respond positively to industrial decline, high levels of unemployment and poor quality of life by providing new opportunities for participants and by raising aspirations and confidence. A majority of learners interviewed by HMI had few or no previous qualifications. These learners are often balancing considerable life issues relating to poverty, child care, difficult family circumstances, and poor health, particularly mental health, with involvement and achievement in CLD programmes. Given this context, the achievements against the national priorities for CLD are significant.

2.1 Outcomes for learners

Overall, effective practice in adult learning and youth work develops individual self-confidence and core skills such as working with others, communication and problem solving. It provides participants with opportunities to learn from experience in those areas of their lives where they choose to learn and often engages their enthusiasm and energy to very good effect. Particularly in youth work, and to a lesser extent in adult learning, the sector needs to use assessment processes more effectively to ensure that participants can identify and build on their learning experiences.

Adult learners in the CLD sector achieve well in a broad range of important outcomes. CLD experiences typically engender great enthusiasm and motivation for learning amongst participants. Staff are particularly effective in developing confidence and self-esteem in the majority of learners who are returning to learning, often following negative experiences of formal education. CLD provision successfully re-introduces them to learning, encouraging them to develop independently their own interests in their studies and at a pace, time and place which suit them. Family learning programmes are increasingly effective in developing interest and aptitude among parents, carers and children in early literacy activities and supporting the work of nurseries and primary schools. In literacy and numeracy work with adults, the majority of learners are developing important capabilities.

---

[24] *Scottish Index of Multiple Deprivation* (SIMD) 2004, Scottish Executive Office of the Chief Statistician, June 2004

Community learning and development 2

PARTICIPANT ACHIEVEMENT

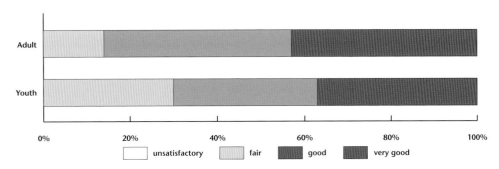

Distribution of quality indicator evaluations in the CLD sector, 2002-2005.

For some, it is not an exaggeration to say that the impact can be life changing.[25] A significant number of adults are gaining employment or progressing to further and higher education as a result of their involvement in adult learning programmes. However, with the exception of the literacies programme, there is insufficient data on the outcomes of adult learning in the community to identify trends in achievement.

Inspections of **youth work** involve meeting young people in traditional youth clubs and centres, on the streets with detached youth workers, in youth award programmes and in projects concerned with youth information, health, youth cultural activities, environmental awareness or citizenship and democracy. Young people are learning important core skills such as communication, working with others, and problem solving. Most participants experience improvements in their self-confidence and self-esteem. In some projects these core skills are supplemented with skills and experiences relevant to future employment.

Citizenship activities, such as youth forums or youth conferences, often result in young people taking more active roles in their communities and advocating on behalf of other young people (see also *Citizenship in Youth Work* (HMIE 2003)). Youth cultural activities build on young people's enthusiasms for music, art, drama and multi-media to develop further their skills in these areas. Youth award programmes provide particularly effective means of engaging young people in project work. These programmes provide effective assessment arrangements and enable young people to recognise and celebrate their successes. However, the availability of this impressive range of opportunities for young people varies considerably across Scotland. With the exception of some award programmes, there is insufficient data on the outcomes of youth work to identify trends in achievement.

---

[25] *Changing Lives: Adult Literacy and Numeracy in Scotland* (HMIE 2005)

2.2 Outcomes for communities

Work in building community capacity is well developed in some of Scotland's more disadvantaged areas where specific funding has supported a mix of initiatives to enable local people to participate fully in programmes to improve their communities. Work remains to be done to improve monitoring and evaluation arrangements for community capacity building in a majority of local authorities.

COMMUNITY ACHIEVEMENT

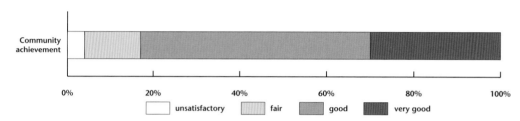

Distribution of quality indicator evaluations in the CLD sector, 2002-2005.

Community capacity building normally involves programmes of training, information and support to enable local people to engage with local and wider issues and to deliver services. Since 2003, CLD providers have become increasingly involved in supporting communities to engage with Community Planning. It is too early to evaluate any impact. However, evidence from inspections identifies a range of community achievements arising from the work of community workers with local people, young and old. In some disadvantaged areas, local people are significantly involved in major regeneration initiatives. Through this involvement they developed their capacity to influence public bodies and local decision making. The most significant outcome from this work is a sense of community ownership of new developments and considerable pride in their achievements. More generally, effective support for community and voluntary organisations resulted in vibrant and active communities.

2.3 The views of learners and participants

In CLD inspections, participants' views of their experience are gathered through focus groups and individual interviews. Learners' views contribute to evaluations of provision. Generally, most of those participating in CLD programmes who had negative previous experiences of education find that these programmes offer them an accessible return to learning.

3. Meeting the needs of all participants

Overall, youth workers and adult tutors develop very positive relationships with the people with whom they are in contact. They generally show a high degree of responsiveness to the needs and preferences of young people and adults and create environments which are sympathetic and supportive. Examples of best practice in the sector demonstrate the effectiveness of the work with particularly disadvantaged and marginalised individuals and groups. Adult tutors usually adopt approaches to facilitating learning which start from participants' learning needs and work towards their individual learning goals. This approach is also adopted in more structured youth work programmes.

3.1 Learning programmes and delivery

Partnership arrangements in adult learning usually result in providers working effectively together to offer flexible programmes on a wide range of subjects. However, in a few areas the level of provision is constrained by lack of resources. Programmes are developed in response to locally identified needs. Provision for young people is more variable across different parts of Scotland and is to some extent influenced by the degree of priority given to it by the local community.

Learning programmes are characterised by a number of key factors, including the following.

- Flexible design, location, organisation and delivery of programmes encourage socially excluded and disadvantaged individuals and groups to engage in learning activities.

- The voluntary nature of attendance and the negotiation of learning activities ensure predominantly positive learning experiences for participants in CLD, with many progressing to further study, obtaining core skills, qualifications, access to employment and an increase in self-confidence.

- Strong collaborative arrangements with a wide range of partners support effective delivery. Partners include libraries, further education colleges, voluntary and community organisations, the enterprise network, health promotion and education, universities, and others.

- CLD staff effectively guide and support learners of all ages at transition points in their education.

LEARNING OPPORTUNITIES/DELIVERY/LEARNING EXPERIENCE

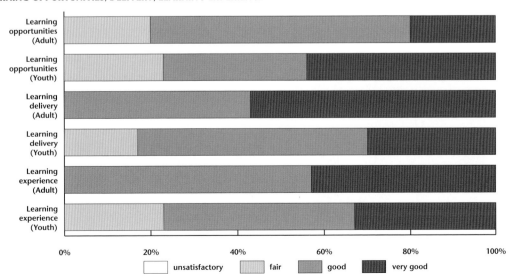

Distribution of quality indicator evaluations in the CLD sector, 2002-2005.

At times, staff's lack of familiarity and expertise in using ICT result in learners not being able to benefit from learning experiences which are enhanced by appropriate applications of new technology. In some cases, weaknesses in staff review, development and training result in staff lacking the confidence and knowledge to provide learners with the help and support they need for a relevant, rich and rewarding learning experience.

>> Signpost to improvement in assessment

Staff:

- *ensure that approaches to assessment and monitoring are consistent and comprehensive;*
- *develop effective means to recognise achievement and attainment on a regular basis; and*
- *ensure that CLD provision is located within SCQF to support learner attainment and progression.*

Assessment and monitoring of outcomes in certificated programmes in adult learning and youth work are strong and well developed. Programmes which are accredited by the Scottish Qualifications Authority (SQA) follow national guidelines. Award schemes which are delivered by youth organisations such as The Duke of Edinburgh's Award and The Prince's Trust, and programmes accredited by the Award Scheme Development and Accreditation Network (ASDAN) are having a positive impact. In community capacity building, the use of funds from European, regeneration or charitable sources results in well-developed monitoring and evaluation systems to measure outcomes for these programmes. However, other aspects of data collection which would provide trend information at national level are not yet in place. Assessment and monitoring arrangements are inconsistently developed across CLD services. This is particularly notable in youth work where assessment needs to be improved in a majority of councils. The sector needs to improve further the collection and presentation of information on the impact of CLD provision on learners' achievements. The systems for recognising the attainment of learners are still developing across partnerships. Use of the Scottish Credit and Qualifications Framework (SCQF) needs to be further developed so that the achievements of, for example, young people on award schemes may be recognised within national qualification frameworks.

Strong **partnerships** enable a wide range of learners to access suitable and flexible learning activities with well-planned progression opportunities. Effective community learning plans are characterised by both strategic and operational staff developing productive partnerships with further education colleges, employers, community and voluntary organisations, and other educational institutions such as universities and schools. There is scope for further improvement in partnership working for adult literacy and numeracy provision. Inspection teams find that where the processes of learning and teaching ensure that learners' needs are specifically addressed and support and guidance for all learners are provided, outcomes and opportunities for progression improve.

Community learning and development 2

3.2 Climate and support

Commitment to **inclusion** is a principle which underpins CLD. In some authorities, the sector is very effective at targeting excluded groups such as lone parents, the unemployed and former drug and alcohol misusers. Programmes of English for Speakers of Other Languages (ESOL) include learners from a wide diversity of backgrounds, including asylum seekers. However, despite the very positive aspects of CLD provision in engaging with socially excluded groups, a number of areas need to receive greater attention and emphasis. Profile information about local communities is often out-of-date and of limited use. This may mean that CLD staff do not have a complete understanding of the demographic characteristics of the communities they work in. Specifically, inspectors come across fewer examples of CLD work with black and minority ethnic individuals and groups, and people with disabilities. Compliance with race equality and disability discrimination legislation needs to become better embedded in service planning and practice and result in improved services for these groups.

VALUES

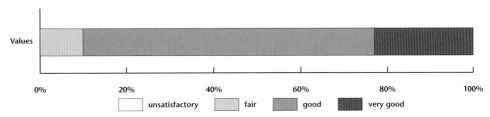

Distribution of quality indicator evaluations in the CLD sector, 2002-2005.

Some important weaknesses in **accommodation** are found in half of all CLD inspections. The range and variety of accommodation is wide and usually includes use of local facilities such as schools, community centres and village and church halls. Overall, activities on offer to learners are responsive to local needs. To ensure inclusive participation, the learning environments and the atmosphere in which participants learn are typically friendly, relaxed, informal, purposeful, and conducive to learning.

However, particularly where services are delivered in older community buildings, access for people with disabilities can be difficult and sometimes impossible. Work with some CLD groups is best undertaken in premises other than schools. In a minority of community venues the environment is drab and uninviting and in many, limited access to ICT equipment is a particular drawback in the context of learning.

ACCOMMODATION AND FACILITIES

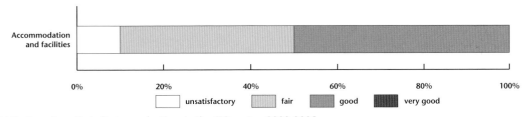

Distribution of quality indicator evaluations in the CLD sector, 2002-2005.

4. Leadership and capacity to improve

4.1 Leadership

LEADERSHIP

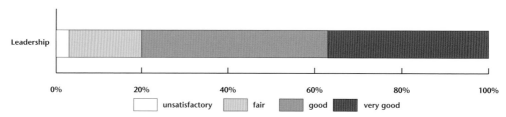

Distribution of quality indicator evaluations in the CLD sector, 2002-2005.

In many geographic areas where CLD is delivered, effective leadership and partnerships at strategic level encourage the development of community learning strategies which provide a clear vision for CLD in the local authority.

From these strategies, local managers and staff are able to develop local plans which identify key outcomes to be achieved and the processes which will achieve them. However, in a fifth of the provision inspected, leadership was evaluated as fair or unsatisfactory. In most cases, the predominant difficulty is the relatively low priority and resources which some local authorities are able to give to CLD strategic planning within the wide range of their other priorities.

The planning context for CLD has changed considerably in the period of this review. The legislative requirement for local authorities to implement Community Planning with key partner agencies and in consultation with communities impacted directly on CLD providers.

Also in this period, the introduction of children's services planning began to have an effect on planning for youth work. In the best examples, strategic planning had significantly improved the extent to which providers worked effectively together, resulting in improved co-ordination and delivery of services in local areas. However, in half the provision inspected, there was a need to clarify strategic and operational planning and particularly to align community learning and development strategies more effectively within Community Planning.

COMMUNITY LEARNING PLANNING

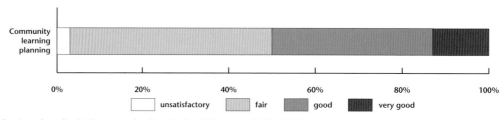

Distribution of quality indicator evaluations in the CLD sector, 2002-2005.

Community learning and development

4.2 Capacity to improve

The period covered by this report began with the publication of the first **self-evaluation** framework for CLD in Scotland, *How good is our community learning and development?*. As with other sectors of education it has taken time for the process of self-evaluation for improvement to become embedded in the sector. The rate of progress has varied widely between authorities. By the end of the review period, a few authorities had produced well-considered standards and quality reports on their CLD provision. The majority, however, were only beginning to recognise the potential benefits of using a systematic approach to self-evaluation for quality improvement.

SELF-EVALUATION/PLANNING FOR IMPROVEMENT

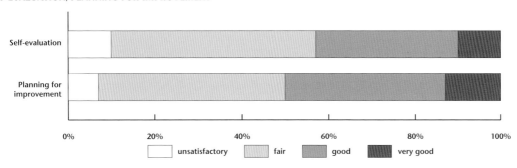

Distribution of quality indicator evaluations in the CLD sector, 2002-2005.

Signpost to improvement in ‹‹
self-evaluation and
planning

Staff:

- *ensure that strategies and plans articulate clearly with one another;*
- *use a planning approach which starts by identifying the intended outcomes and impact;*
- *develop performance information systems which provide benchmark data for year-on-year improvement;*
- *build in self-evaluation processes from the start; and*
- *use self-evaluation tools which suit the local circumstances.*

The weaknesses in CLD providers' quality assurance and improvement arrangements often relate to:

- insufficient use of recruitment, retention and progression information in the evaluation of programmes and in future planning;

- insufficient or ineffective processes to identify, learn from, and replicate good practice both within and across local authorities; and

- failure to extend the effective arrangements for quality assurance and improvement in some aspects of provision, such as adult literacy and numeracy, to other areas.

To date, HMIE has undertaken 11 follow-up reviews of the CLD services inspected in the period 2002-2005. The follow-up reports reveal that in nearly all cases CLD providers had made good or very good progress in addressing almost all main points for action.

The CLD sector is complex and varied. At national level it is informed by three main strands of Scottish Executive policy. Those currently in place are the lifelong learning strategy and the community regeneration statement. The third main strand, the national youth work strategy, is currently subject to development. At local authority level, CLD providers are starting to contribute to children's services plans and the community engagement aspects of Community Planning. Service structures for CLD vary considerably across Scotland in response to local circumstances and priorities. CLD strategies are now in place in almost all community planning partnerships. The national priorities for CLD contained within the guidance *Working and Learning Together to Build Stronger Communities* provide a common focus for articulating local purposes and priorities.

Community learning and development 2

The 2002-2005 inspection programme highlighted many strengths within the sector during a period of, perhaps, unprecedented change. It also highlighted some important areas for action and development. Over this period, a number of authorities have made significant progress since previous inspections of their community learning provision. A few, however, still have considerable scope for improvement. The sector needs to develop the collection and use of performance information, the use of self-evaluation for quality improvement, and aspects of strategic and operational planning. Given progress in these areas, and with appropriate national and local support, the CLD sector has the capacity to improve further.

Section Three: Major themes and significant issues

This section draws on evidence gathered through the full range of HMIE activities. In doing so, it does not seek to be a comprehensive summary of the sector reports, nor does it comment on every aspect of Scottish education.

3.1 School curriculum

HMIE evaluations indicate that the **quality of the structure of the curriculum** in primary and secondary schools is good overall. These evaluations were made against a backdrop of an agreed set of curriculum guidelines, broadly accepted by society and by schools as meeting the needs of most learners. However, recent and continuing societal and technological changes now present new needs and challenges. The curriculum must evolve to meet learners' and society's needs in the less certain world of the 21st century. The Scottish Executive, through acceptance of the principles in *A Curriculum for Excellence* and supported by the advice in the national priorities for schools, has begun that process.

Recently, awareness in schools of the need for the curriculum to be appropriate for individual learners has become more acute. A number of schools have engaged in small-scale or large-scale **curricular change**. In some cases they have successfully and appropriately adapted the curriculum. They have based changes on a well-considered rationale, consulted stakeholders appropriately, monitored implementation closely and are evaluating the impact of the changes. Many of those schools have thus developed a more relevant curriculum for groups of pupils, resulting in improvements in pupils' learning, attitudes and achievements. Other schools have embarked on change without sufficient preparation, thereby risking pupils' educational outcomes. Neither have they necessarily sought to find out and address, before embarking on alternative programmes, weaknesses in learning and teaching which might lie behind pupils' disengagement from the mainstream curriculum.

STRUCTURE OF THE CURRICULUM

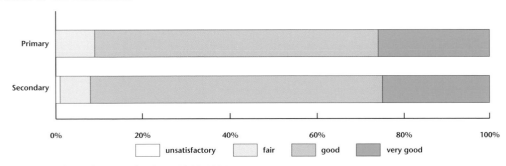

Distribution of quality indicator evaluations, 2002-2005.

In a considerable number of cases in secondary schools, changes to the curriculum have related to increasing the extent of **vocational education** provided for lower-attaining groups of pupils, often through school-college partnerships. Some schools are not alert enough to the need to balance positive aspects of increased vocational education with the risk of shutting off alternative futures at too early a stage. Conversely, although there are signs that some schools are providing vocational enhancements for higher-attaining pupils, few schools have systematic arrangements for increased vocational education for all.

Attention to the national priorities for school education has led to education authorities and many primary and secondary schools improving access to activities outwith the formal curriculum. Study support, homework clubs, out-of-hours learning, summer schools, primary-secondary liaison, residential outdoor activities and eco activities have all been promoted. Education authorities and schools have also been encouraged to address cross-curricular aspects such as education for enterprise and citizenship.

Schools increasingly understand the potential impact of enterprise in education on young people's experiences. The range and depth of business involvement has improved and levels of awareness have been raised. However, there remains a need to develop more opportunities for pupils and more varied learning and teaching approaches which develop pupils' enterprise skills in both primary and secondary school contexts.

Schools also have increased their emphasis on citizenship. Many are giving some more attention to involving young people in decision making. Some have used curriculum inserts to explore issues such as citizenship and the law or anti-racism. However, practice is uneven within and across schools. The development of pupils' understanding of values and citizenship, including the ability to hold informed views and make judgements, depends on the acquisition of knowledge and critical thinking skills. Systematic curriculum planning to ensure that pupils are well prepared for political, social, economic and cultural involvement in society and to participate in significant decisions at school is not yet common.

As schools develop citizenship further, they need to ensure that values associated with responsible citizenship are also promoted through pupils' everyday classroom experiences and the life of the school as a community.

3.2 Achievement

The terms 'achievement' and 'attainment' are both used in the Scottish educational context in connection with learner outcomes. Attainment, as an indication of levels of performance in assessment and qualifications contexts, is of critical importance. However, it cannot be the only measure of success. Some indication of the broader personal outcomes associated with the learning and development of the 'all-round' individual is also required. HMIE uses 'achievement' as the overarching term which includes both attainment in qualifications and success in those broader aspects.

Sector reports in Section 2 identify a number of strengths in educational outcomes in national and international contexts. They highlight many positive indicators in terms of the overall quality of learners' attainment. However, there is still significant room for improvement. For example, progress in attainment is uneven at different stages, across different educational establishments, within individual establishments and for different groups of learners.

The various ways in which attainment in Scottish education has been accredited and certificated have, in the last quarter of the 20th century, been largely successful in the context of the curriculum of the day. Scottish qualifications are held in high esteem internationally.

The establishment of 5-14 levels of attainment against which to assess individual progress provided an improved framework for progression but one which teachers found difficult to implement fully beyond English language and mathematics. Approaches to allow schools to benchmark pupils' performances and share standards across all areas of the curriculum, with a view to improving pupils' learning and achievement, should be found and developed.

Certification at Standard Grade was particularly successful in allowing almost all learners to be accredited for what they had achieved. The more recent national qualifications introduced for all learners at the post-S4 stage have provided new opportunities for them to have their learning accredited, whether they are in secondary school, special school or college.

However, our qualifications system has been developed piecemeal over the last 25 years, focusing at different times on different stages of education, often in tandem with relevant curricular changes. In addition, some qualifications in certain subjects are now, for various reasons, outdated.

>> *Signpost to improvement in achievement*

Teachers/responsible adults:

- *promote a 'can do' culture of achievement in learning situations;*
- *give learners tasks which are achievable but challenging for them;*
- *motivate learners through learning activities or exploit motivations which learners already have;*
- *sensitively show examples of good work by other learners;*
- *negotiate with learners specific and appropriate targets and track progress towards them – in individual lessons, over the short term and in the longer term;*
- *demonstrate interest both in learners' attainment and broader achievements;*
- *are aware of learners' achievements beyond the formal learning situation;*
- *recognise those positive achievements which may not be overt and obvious; and*
- *praise progress and celebrate success appropriately.*

Scottish schools provide opportunities, through what is currently known as 'extra-curricular' or sometimes 'out-of-school' activities, for pupils to develop skills, aptitudes and positive attributes across a range of contexts. These include sport, the creative arts, community and charity work, intellectual pursuits and many others. Some such activities encourage pupils to stretch themselves and face personal challenges or to extend horizons by engaging with broader human, global and environmental issues. Some are recognised formally, while others, including those offered in many special schools, make important contributions to pupils' personal and social development in ways which are difficult to measure. School efforts are extended by activities offered through CLD providers. FE colleges also increase the range of experiences offered to learners through, for example, life skills programmes and citizenship-related activities such as voluntary work, enhancement activities including study or trips abroad and participation in competitions related to learners' areas of study.

If the ambitious aspirations set out for young people in Scotland are to be realised, action is required to formalise many such arrangements. Education authorities and schools, working with CLD staff, should find ways of bringing such activities more into the mainstream of provision for all learners, rather than leave them as part of 'extra-curricular' activities which depend on the good will of staff.

Current initial developments in tracking learners' activities and in recording, accrediting and celebrating their achievements need to be encouraged and promoted. *A Curriculum for Excellence,* with its focus on education from 3 to 18, presents a unique opportunity to take a more holistic view not only of the curriculum, but also of assessment and qualifications procedures and the accreditation of broader aspects of achievement.

3.3 Learning

Learning demands for life in the 21st century are very different from those required in former times. The reality and complexity of global, social, scientific and technological change require education to provide learners with more than knowledge and understanding. Amongst the core skills with which it must also equip them is the **skill of learning** itself. Education must teach learners how to learn. It must also teach them how to access safely and successfully the huge volume of information and knowledge now available through new technologies. Section 2 sector reports attest to some green shoots in the promotion of the skill of learning, but also highlight this aspect as one for improvement.

LEARNING EXPERIENCES

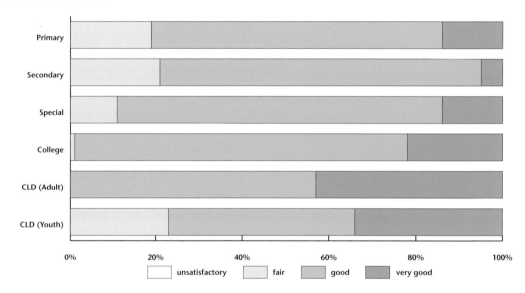

Distribution of quality indicator evaluations. Note that college figures relate to the quality of learning and teaching as a single indicator.

In the last few years, teachers in the school and college sectors have begun to promote among learners a greater understanding of the learning process. For example, many colleges have stimulated a greater degree of learners' engagement, through seeking and acting on their views of their learning experiences. Many schools do not as yet involve pupils sufficiently in discussions about the quality of their learning experiences. However, the extent to which pupils are being helped towards an understanding of how they learn *has* increased. This is often helpful, but is likely to be counterproductive if it leads to the exclusive adoption by either learner or teacher of any one approach to learning.

More generally, while there are considerable strengths in the quality of young peoples' learning, leading to many positive outcomes across all sectors, further improvement is needed. Often the pace of learning is too slow or too variable. Activities offered should be challenging enough to promote progress and be designed well enough for learners to experience success and achieve worthwhile outcomes. More frequent opportunities are required for learners to be actively involved in learning activities as individuals or co-operatively in small groups. Tasks and activities do not frequently enough ask learners to think creatively and respond confidently and imaginatively to new challenges, learning how to overcome obstacles in their way. Improvements could also be achieved in the extent to which learners' skills in learning itself are promoted and enhanced as they move across and through different sectors of education. Scottish education is successful in ensuring learners' care and welfare and, to some extent, in improving the coherence of their curriculum content at points of transition. Arrangements to ensure the quality of transition from year to year or sector to sector as far as learning is concerned are less secure and more variable in quality.

Supporting learners, enhancing their motivation to succeed, providing focus for their learning, and preparing them to give evidence of their learning all contribute to improving outcomes. In addition, careful tracking and monitoring of their performance and attention to their progress supports them in their achievements. The system needs to ensure that those most requiring this support, particularly groups of learners among the lowest-attaining 20%, are sensitively identified and supported to achieve worthwhile outcomes.

3.4 Ethos and behaviour

Inspection evidence indicates that the overall climate and ethos within pre-school centres, schools, colleges and CLD contexts is good and often very good.

While this is so, teachers in schools report that indiscipline is growing. HMIE recently published a report on this complex issue, entitled *A Climate for Learning* (HMIE 2005).
The report concluded that most Scottish children behave well at school. Despite heightened challenges, most schools have made good progress in sustaining a cycle of positive behaviour and effective learning within a context of greater commitment to the inclusion of pupils who are less easy to motivate and engage. Nevertheless, meeting the needs of some children should not be at the expense of meeting the needs of all. It is important to recognise that, for complex reasons which often go well beyond the influence of the school, there are some major breakdowns of discipline with serious consequences. The extent of such breakdowns may be reduced by effective inter-agency working and appropriate levels of behaviour support.

In addition, low-level disruptive behaviour is not infrequently a significant problem in individual classes or departments, with an adverse effect on learning. There is strong evidence that there are clear links between low-level indiscipline and factors such as the quality of the curriculum, courses and programmes of study, learning activities, and the ways in which learners' successes are recognised. Indiscipline should not be treated in isolation from the curriculum and from learning experiences. Improvements are achievable where learning is focused, active and practical, with built-in milestones to encourage recognition of progress, appropriate and supportive interim assessment and suitable end-point recognition. Improvements are also achievable through common approaches from teachers and from senior staff within the context of a strong and consistently applied positive behaviour policy.

Linked to ethos and behaviour, and also to inclusion and citizenship, is the issue of bullying. In school inspections, HMI seek pupils' views on bullying and form a view on the quality both of the way the school develops pupils' awareness and of the arrangements the school makes to deal with reported instances. Despite overall very positive efforts by most schools, a few serious

>> *Signpost to improvement in inclusion*

- *The effectiveness of inclusive education is closely linked to sound leadership, high-quality learning and teaching, and imaginative use of curriculum flexibility to meet learners' diverse needs.*

- *Disruptive and disaffected learners are more effectively included where behaviour management policies are clear and consistently implemented, and where success is celebrated.*

- *Some of the best inclusive practice takes place where learners have access to appropriate resources, specialist support staff and on-site bases, all designed to keep school-age learners included in mainstream education.*

- *Positive influences on meeting learners' needs are more likely to occur through the broader agenda possible when services for children and young people work together.*

- *Benefits to school-aged learners can accrue when care is taken, in the context of the use of off-site centres, to ensure that pupils' progress is supported and recorded, links are maintained with the 'home school' and opportunities remain open for regular reintegration as appropriate in mainstream education contexts.*

- *At key stages of transfer, learners' needs are more likely to be addressed effectively where teachers have access to relevant information relating to achievement, curriculum and learning as well as pastoral aspects.*

instances may occur, with, at times, very serious consequences. Continued efforts are required by all, in partnership with other agencies as necessary, to deal effectively with the issue.

3.5 Meeting the needs of all learners

Inclusion

The expansion of pre-school education has contributed positively to a more supported start to education for many children. In particular, it has brought many vulnerable children into a context of care and education at a stage in their life where intervention can make a significant difference.

Many establishments in all sectors and many local authorities have strengthened their

MEETING NEEDS

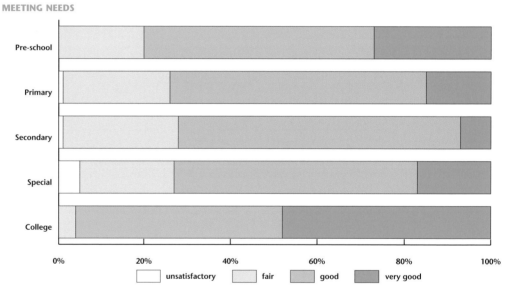

Distribution of quality indicator evaluations. Note that college figures relate to individual subject areas, not the college as a whole. In the CLD sector, meeting needs is evaluated as part of learning experiences.

policies on diversity, equality and fairness. Partly in response to legislation, approaches to promoting race equality and equal opportunities for disabled people are in the process of being reviewed and improved. Overall, there is an increased awareness of the needs of vulnerable minority groups such as Gypsy Travellers, asylum seekers and looked after, and looked after and accommodated, children and young people. Colleges generally make good provision for all learners, while CLD services offer learning opportunities for some of the most socially disadvantaged groups. Overall, Scottish education has made significant progress towards a more inclusive education system.

The nature and quality of the implementation of inclusive approaches, however, remains variable across the country, particularly in the schools' sectors. Barriers to pupils' achievements in the education system, which may emerge from the cycle of low expectations associated with social disadvantage, are still clearly evident across Scotland (see *Missing Out* (HMIE 2006)).

Development of the integrated community schooling approach has been one major strategy for promoting greater inclusiveness (see *The Sum of its Parts* (HMIE 2004)).

Although progress has been variable, there are promising signs of what the approach can offer. It has helped raise awareness of the importance of partnership and inter-agency working to promote achievement and improve social inclusion. Equally, movement towards inter-agency working at strategic level in local authorities, especially within the context of Integrated Children's Services, has increased.

Despite some improvements in inter-agency working, arrangements for funding and accountability have been too fragmented and have not always been successful in promoting effective joint actions. Across all sectors, there remains a need for multi-disciplinary staff development.

In addition, baseline data and strategies for recording, reporting and monitoring the progress of learners in a range of minority groups needs to be improved. Arrangements for ensuring continuity of learning for learners with interrupted education often need to be developed further to prevent them slipping through the net.

Promoting the good health and well-being of learners

The education system can and should make a major contribution to encouraging healthy living. Lifestyle choices, including lack of exercise and poor diet, are significant contributors to Scotland's unenviable health record. The Scottish Executive expects all schools to be working towards **Health Promoting Schools** status by the end of 2007. Ways to increase the physical activity of children and young people are explored in the Scottish Executive's *The Report of the Physical Education Review Group* (June 2004). Only a long-term view and consideration of health statistics in years to come will indicate whether such measures have had a significant impact. In the meantime, a number of comments can be made.

Good progress is being made in implementing the recommendations of *Hungry for Success* to improve school meals and related aspects particularly in primary schools. Schools increasingly work closely with partner agencies and parents to deliver key aspects of education about sensitive issues including sexual health and drugs education. An increasing number of colleges and especially CLD providers now work in partnership with health professionals in initiatives to promote health among young people and adults. The involvement of partner agencies and engagement of parents in health education programmes still needs to be improved.

Schools are generally aware of the expectations arising from the review of physical education. A number of local authorities and schools are working on the practical implications and some pilot projects are underway. To date, the pace of implementation of the recommendation that pupils should have two hours of good quality physical education per week has been slow.

Outwith formal education, opportunities are offered, through school or community clubs, for example, or through the work of Active Schools Co-ordinators, for children and young people to engage in energetic physical activities. However, many who might benefit choose not to opt in. This applies particularly to girls. Overall, the challenge of increasing children's levels of activity, from an early age and throughout their education, must be taken up if Scotland's health is to improve.

Keeping children safe: child protection issues

Pre-school centres, schools, colleges and education authorities have taken positive steps in the last few years to ensure that all teachers and support staff have received training in the handling of child protection issues.

As a first step towards the full inspection of Services for Children, a joint inspection team led by HMIE carried out two pilot inspections into child protection arrangements in two authorities in early 2005. Strengths identified by the pilot inspections included improvements in joint working between professionals and agencies at strategic and operational levels, the important role played by voluntary sector organisations working alongside statutory agencies and the commitment of professionals whose core task was child protection.

While still at a very early stage in the inspection of child protection, some key issues emerged which need to be reviewed by all those concerned with the welfare of safety of children and young people. These included the need to:

- ensure that children and young people are more actively involved in decision making and have the right to be heard;

- improve arrangements for assessing risks and needs and support this by improved record keeping;

- improve information sharing across agencies and services; and

- improve quality assurance arrangements in order to evaluate the effectiveness of the work of agencies both singly and collectively.

3.6 Staffing, teaching and professional responsibility

Staffing

Scotland is at the forefront internationally with regard to the extent to which our teaching force is professionally qualified. Furthermore, all our nursery nurses and technicians and an increasing number of adults who support teaching, such as classroom assistants, have relevant qualifications. Overall, teaching staff are very competent in many aspects of their work and are almost always hard-working and committed to their learners. Teachers across all sectors address well the care and welfare of children, young people and adults.

The staffing situation in pre-school is very varied in terms of the level of qualification of individual members of staff. While the level of qualifications is increasing overall, around a quarter of staff have no formal childcare qualifications. Many children do not have regular contact with a qualified teacher in learning contexts.

Teacher Education Institutions (TEIs) are experiencing some difficulties in finding school placements for all students. It is essential for the continued health of education that schools and education authorities accept training responsibilities for the future generation of teachers.

The decisions of the implementation group of the Committee of Inquiry into Professional Conditions of Service for Teachers (The McCrone Committee, 1999) were set out in *A Teaching Profession for the 21st Century* (The Teachers' Agreement) and were to be phased in over a period up to 2006. Among the issues addressed were new career structures for teaching and non-teaching staff, continuing professional development and arrangements for newly-qualified teachers. HMIE, along with Audit Scotland, is currently engaged in long-term monitoring of the implementation of the Agreement. HMIE will produce a report later in 2006. Firm conclusions as to outcomes and impact on learning ahead of that report would be premature. There are positive signs relating to some aspects, such as the appointment of professional business managers in secondary schools or clusters of schools, the developing role of classroom assistants, support for newly-qualified teachers and continuing professional development arrangements. Whilst progress is being made in line with agreed timescales to implement new staffing arrangements and structures, there remains scope to improve the impact on the quality of experience of children and young people.

Teaching

Teaching staff in all sectors manage learning opportunities well and plan appropriately for the delivery of lesson content. Often they are well supported in the teaching process by other adults and professionals. A growing number of teachers are developing a broader understanding of the role of assessment within learning and the potential of discussing learning itself to motivate and empower learners.

Increasingly the range of approaches used by teachers includes ICT applications. However, many teachers still need to extend their competences in using technology appropriately in learning and teaching. Young people live in an electronic age – not to recognise that and include the appropriate use of ICT as part of learning sends powerful messages about relevance and the usefulness of education to learners. We also need to ensure that all learners develop appropriate information literacy skills which support them in their current and future personal lives as well as in work contexts. The HMIE report *The integration of information and communications technology in Scottish schools* (HMIE 2005) offers a current evaluation with a view to supporting national improvement.

Professional responsibility

Every teacher, in whatever sector, can work towards improving the quality of the learning which their learners experience, the teaching which supports it and the outcomes which their learners achieve. At the core of that improvement lie self-evaluation, observing examples of other approaches, discussing with colleagues, being open to well-judged innovation, learning from research, undertaking action research and fully engaging in making education fit for purpose in the 21st century. A key pre-requisite is that teachers accept responsibility for their own professional development, for the quality of learning in their classrooms, and for their role in self-evaluation and improvement at personal and establishment levels. Many teachers fulfil these responsibilities, but some do not.

The greatest impact for improvement comes through work in individual classrooms or learning contexts, whatever the sector. To allow teaching staff to do their job effectively and fulfil their key role in improvement, support, in the context of continuing professional development, must be available. Some new support mechanisms are now opening up. Tapping in to opportunities offered through ICT to access good practice should be promoted and encouraged. Overall, the Scottish Executive and all agencies involved in supporting improvement, including HMIE, need to ensure that educational establishments and individual staff members have ready technological and professional access to good quality support, research information and examples of good established practice and innovative practices. Teachers for their part need to respond positively to the opportunities offered.

3.7 Leadership, change and accountability

Effective leadership, in pre-school or community settings, schools or colleges, impacts strongly on the quality of learning, teaching and achievement as well as being instrumental in creating a vibrant culture and sense of community. Increasingly, leadership is being viewed as a corporate concept which relates not only to the head of establishment but also to the combined impact of all those who have responsibility for leading any aspect of provision for learners. The head is ultimately accountable in terms of the quality of education within the establishment and of the resulting progress made by learners. Leadership is therefore both individual and shared. Leadership has major strengths in around two out of every five educational establishments in Scotland, although there is some variation across sectors.

>> *Signpost to improvement in professional responsibility*

Teaching staff:

- *focus on issues to do with learning and teaching in staff development time;*
- *keep their professional knowledge (subject, pedagogy, ICT applications) up-to-date;*
- *are aware of research implications and seek to apply them as relevant in personal action research;*
- *consider how, as individual teachers, they can promote the development of successful learners, confident individuals, effective contributors and responsible citizens;*
- *gather the views of their learners about the quality of learning experiences and progress and act on findings;*
- *recognise that they, too, are learners; and*
- *have access to high-quality staff development.*

LEADERSHIP

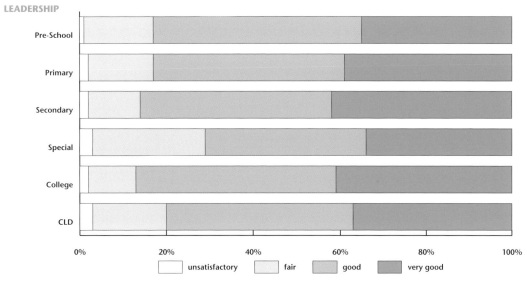

Distribution of quality indicator evaluations. In colleges, the data refer to educational leadership and direction.

Chart legend: unsatisfactory | fair | good | very good

Y-axis categories: Pre-School, Primary, Secondary, Special, College, CLD

X-axis: 0%, 20%, 40%, 60%, 80%, 100%

In many cases, the head of establishment is hard-working, demonstrates a range of qualities and is successful in creating and maintaining a positive environment for learning. Across the pre-school, school, college and CLD sectors, many heads are good at establishing partnerships with other relevant agencies and thereby enhancing learning, support or progression opportunities. Amongst the leaders who are very good, some stand out as having an ability to inspire learners and staff, a capacity to 'see over the horizon' and the energy to sustain long-term improvement.

Appropriately, in the context of shared leadership, a greater number of heads are giving staff in different teaching or management roles opportunities to lead projects, work together on agreed tasks and share their good practice. Increasing attention is being paid to learners' views and to the use of performance data to identify good practice, highlight underachievement and target support on greatest need.

However, such improvements are not evident across the board. In some instances heads need to develop a culture which sustains collaborative working and empowers other staff to become leaders in their own areas (including in the classroom). There is a need, especially in pre-school centres, for roles and responsibilities of all staff to be clear and well communicated to all. Across all sectors, some heads have an inadequate strategic overview or do not monitor appropriately the progress of initiatives or changes and their impact on learners. In all contexts throughout the education system, there is scope for improvement in the extent to which leaders focus on learners and learning.

Since the early 1990s, educational establishments have made great strides in becoming aware of their own strengths and weaknesses and planning for and effecting improvement in their work. This represents a major step forward, with establishments taking responsibility for driving their own quality improvement rather than relying on outside agencies to do this for them.

>> *Signpost to improvement in leadership (2)*

Good leadership:

- *is appropriately consultative in style, with teamwork valued and developed;*
- *is shared and distributed, allowing staff at all levels to be given opportunities to lead projects, work together and take responsibility;*
- *allows for learners to be consulted and involved; and*
- *promotes the use of performance data to identify good practice, target under-achievement and support those in need of additional assistance.*

Now, in all sectors, established self-evaluation processes require to move on to a more advanced plane. Generally, across all sectors, heads need to ensure that self-evaluation leads to improvements in provision. In too many cases, self-evaluation can become almost an end in itself. Too often judgements about effectiveness are based on staff views alone. For improvements to occur and be sustained, heads must engage in measured and effective self-evaluation, using performance data and stakeholders' views and ensuring that resulting actions impact on the important features of provision which require attention.

SELF-EVALUATION

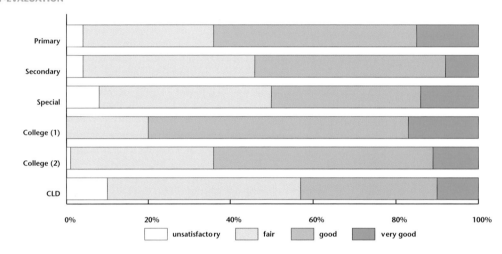

Distribution of quality indicator evaluations. College (1) figures are those for Quality Improvement at college level; College (2) figures are those for Quality Assurance and Improvement at programme team level.

In a very small number of instances, inspectors find educational establishments where the quality of leadership, ethos, provision, learning and outcomes for learners have major weaknesses. The number of such cases has reduced over the last few decades. Improvements in accountability processes and the extent of support and challenge, for example from education authorities, have generally ensured an earlier identification of difficulties and intervention to promote change and improvement. However, any instance of an establishment in difficulties is one too many, affecting, as it does, the experiences and life chances of individual children and learners. Recognition of the severity of problems is a first step towards acceptance that change is needed and that help is required.

3.8 The national context: policy into practice

The Scottish Executive is responding to changed and changing demographic, technological and social circumstances. It has drawn up policies and instigated initiatives designed to support learners and improve the outcomes they achieve, within an inclusive and integrated Scottish context. This sub-section comments briefly on some of the key national policies which have influenced the direction of provision in schools, college and CLD sectors.

Lifelong learning

The Scottish Executive has set out its lifelong learning strategy in *Life Through Learning: Learning Through Life* (SE 2003). It defines lifelong learning as being *'about personal fulfilment and enterprise; employability and adaptability; and active citizenship and social inclusion'*. The strategy deals predominantly with the post-school sectors but encompasses areas of school provision. Guidance produced in February 2004 in *Working and Learning Together to Build Stronger Communities* placed a requirement on local authorities to lead the development of new community learning and development strategies within a Community Planning framework. Policies for the schools sectors, in particular as set out in *Ambitious, Excellent Schools* and in the Executive's response to *Determined to Succeed* are also relevant to lifelong learning.

Colleges provide effective support and guidance into future employment for their learners, whether directly from further education or after higher education. They are largely successful in offering planned progression routes and providing work experience placements and assignments which give learners a taste of specific areas of study or employment. In colleges generally, provision has continued to focus increasingly strongly on learners developing employability skills, with many colleges building some particularly effective links with some industries, businesses and trades.

Working and Learning Together to Build Stronger Communities articulated three new national priorities for CLD: achievement through learning for young people; achievement through learning for adults; and achievement through building community capacity. A clear impact of the guidance has been to raise the profile of CLD in terms of community planning and generally underline the contribution of a sector which can offer a broad range of learning experiences and opportunities for community involvement to young people and adults. There have been successes in establishing partnerships to ensure that service providers for more disadvantaged individuals and groups work well together. There has not yet been time for any significant progress in achievement to be apparent.

Aspects of lifelong learning as defined in the strategy have begun to make a mark on provision and opportunities for school learners. For example, though it is as yet too early to make clear evaluative comments on any impact on learner outcomes, activities related to enterprise in education are now better established in many schools. There is also an increasing focus on some aspects of vocational education provided through partnerships between schools and other providers, notably colleges. These are beginning to increase learners' awareness of enterprise and the kinds of skills young people need to take into the world of work. In many cases, improvements are needed in planning, selection of programmes, communication, and monitoring procedures for attendance and progress of learners. There have been particular successes in the context of helping young people with additional support needs to access and transfer from school to college. The report *Moving On* (HMIE 2003) attests to good practice in both sectors, often supported by input from CLD providers.

The *Standards in Scotland's Schools etc (2000) Act* and the national priorities for education in schools

The *Standards in Scotland's Schools etc (2000) Act* placed a legislative duty on education authorities to secure the development of the *'personality, talents and mental and physical abilities of the child or young person to their fullest potential'.* To achieve this end the Scottish Executive set out a vision for Scotland's children placing the child at the centre of service provision. The vision recognises the need for all children to be safe, nurtured, healthy, achieving, active, included, respected and responsible. It requires agencies and services to collaborate in information sharing, joint planning and effective co-ordinated delivery. It brings together local authorities, police forces, National Health Service Boards and other local partners in planning services for children and families at a local level. The delivery of high-quality services will have an increased emphasis on outcomes achieved for the child and family. At a national level the proposals in *Getting it Right for Every Child* (SE 2003) promote improved assessment and information sharing. An integrated system of inspection of services for children will support improvements across children's services and evaluate the impact of the strategy. These new inspections will begin by 2008.

The 2000 Act also heralded the introduction of national priorities for school education. After consultation with education authorities and others, five national priorities were agreed in December 2000. They relate to: achievement and attainment; framework for learning; inclusion and equality; values and citizenship; and learning for life. There is encouraging evidence that the introduction of national priorities has successfully broadened the agenda for Scottish education. As part of the drive for an inclusive education in which all pupils develop *'to their fullest potential'* and the needs of all are met, curriculum flexibility and the promotion of positive behaviour have had a high priority. The national priorities also set specific outcome measures by which to judge performance. This aspect has been less successful because of weaknesses in some outcome measures.

National priorities have informed improvement planning at the national and local levels and provided a measure of stability and continuity. They have encouraged greater consistency and articulation. They have also provided a way of managing initiatives and funding streams to support the delivery of sustainable improvement in outcomes for learners. Several education authorities have managed the implementation of a range of initiatives by linking them to, and embedding them in, national priority implementation.

Overall, national priorities have had a positive impact on Scottish education. However, the national priorities for schools exist alongside other current and recently introduced measures, strategies and initiatives, such as the inspection of education authorities; curriculum flexibility; *Determined to Succeed;* The Teachers' Agreement and, most recently, *Ambitious, Excellent Schools.* With these and other factors, it is difficult to determine a direct causal link between the national priorities and any measurable improvements in overall performance. A new look at the national priorities could now provide an opportunity to achieve more simplified and streamlined approaches, particularly in the new context of integrated children's services planning.

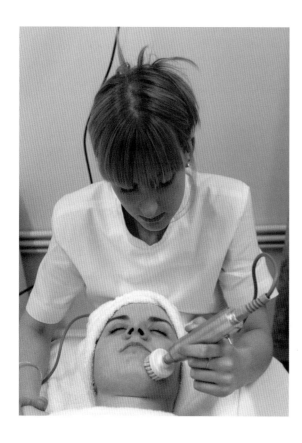

Inspection and improvement

Some time after publication of a report, HMIE returns to establishments and services which have been inspected. The purpose of these follow-through return visits is to determine the extent of progress made. Many establishments and services make considerable progress, and this is documented in follow-through reports. Recently, in the context of proportionate inspection, arrangements for follow-through visits have changed. HMIE now works in close partnership with local authorities in school and CLD inspections, with authorities taking on more responsibility in follow-through activities. Partnership working is an increasing feature of inspection, for example involving Audit Scotland, the Care Commission and other agencies. In the college sector, HMIE works under the terms of a memorandum of understanding with the Scottish Further and Higher Education Funding Council. This commits both bodies to work in partnership to promote continuous quality improvement and enhancement across the sector.

Evidence from establishments responding to HMIE reports highlights some common factors which support improvement.

What works?

A pre-requisite for sustained improvement is recognition by all staff that there is indeed a need for improvement, and that improvement is possible. Successful change needs a number of factors to be in place. When staff accept advice and support positively and commit themselves to collaborating actively in the change process, there is likely to be a very positive impact. Giving learning and teaching the highest priority results in improvements in ethos, behaviour, and outcomes for learners.

In those few school establishments where inspection identified weak or unsatisfactory provision and overall cause for concern, the key to achieving progress has often been a transformation in leadership. That transformation can be effected by a change of headteacher or by a change in the approach of the headteacher in post. In either circumstance, what works is fresh insight, the building of new relationships and partnerships and the introduction of improvement strategies, all within the context of shared leadership and under the overall direction of the headteacher. Acceptance of the need to change and an enthusiastic response to the support offered are pre-requisites in these cases too.

>> *Signpost to overall improvement*

- *Increase levels of visibility of senior staff around the establishment.*
- *Revise remits for senior staff allowing them to focus more on learning and teaching.*
- *Access and apply relevant good practice from other sources.*
- *Focus on improvements to learning and teaching.*
- *Improve whole-establishment systems for communication.*
- *Particularly in the schools sectors, ensure consistent responses to behaviour issues, adopt positive behaviour strategies and recognise the links with the curriculum, learning contexts and learning activities.*
- *Devolve more decision making to drive forward improvement initiatives.*
- *Strengthen self-evaluation systems, processes and outcomes.*
- *Engage learners in the improvement process.*
- *Focus on improvement activities which are outcome-directed, manageable and achievable.*

4

In search of excellence

These follow-through findings are contributing significantly to HMIE's work in relation to *Ambitious, Excellent Schools*. HMIE is aiming to provide practical ideas and support in response to the complex issue of 'what works' in bringing about excellence in the school and pre-school sectors. Drawing on a range of evidence from inspection, from Scottish and international research and from views expressed by stakeholders such as pupils, parents, partner agencies and school staff, HMIE has derived ten characteristics, or dimensions, of excellent pre-school centres and schools. The approach, which suggests that the search for excellence is a continuous journey, is based on the premise that the priority for most schools in Scotland is to improve their currently 'good' practice through 'very good' to 'excellent'. In parallel with this development, HMIE has introduced a new six-point scale for quality indicators with a new level of 'excellent'. These developments will provide establishments with a picture of what they may aim for in their journey towards excellence. In the next *Improving Scottish Education*, HMIE will report on the extent to which excellence is being achieved.

Similar initiatives, for example the quality enhancement themes established by the Scottish Higher and Further Education Funding Council (SFC) for the college sector, also aim to promote and secure practice and learner outcomes at the highest possible levels.

Looking ahead

This report identifies real strengths in Scottish education alongside areas which are priorities for improvement. The drive to raise standards and quality for all learners in all sectors must be sustained. As part of that drive existing measures of attainment should be extended to include broader achievements. Many improvements can be made by individual establishments and their staff. Equally, many will require the active engagement of a wider range of bodies and agencies.

HMIE will support national and local bodies as they consider the implications of this report for their work. For our own part, we will ensure that inspection, review and the other activities of HMIE also address the issues raised in the report. These issues include the following.

Achievement

- continuing to raise standards of attainment for all learners

- promoting and recognising broader achievement more explicitly

- ensuring that the ways in which we recognise achievement, including formal qualifications, reinforce the purposes of the curriculum

Curriculum, Learning and Teaching

- ensuring that the curriculum provides deep, sustained and valuable learning for all learners

- sharpening the focus on the development of essential life skills, particularly literacy and numeracy, for all learners

- maintaining a clear focus on learning and teaching of the highest quality

- using approaches to learning and teaching which promote the development of learners' capacities as described in *A Curriculum for Excellence*

- giving individual establishments and their staff greater scope to exercise their professional roles

4

Inclusion

- enhancing the achievement of our most vulnerable learners

- establishing effective partnership working across children's services

- addressing purposefully issues of equality and diversity

Underperformance

- tackling with greater determination underperformance in meeting the needs of learners

Leadership and Innovation

- promoting leadership of the highest quality which is creative and aspirational and which is unstinting in the pursuit of quality

- building capacity for leadership at all levels

Accountability

- ensuring that our systems of accountability, notably inspection and review, are efficient, complement each other well and contribute to tangible improvement

Appendix

Note on evidence sources and the use of terms

Evidence base

HMIE views as expressed in this report arise from consideration and reflection on a range of factors. These include:

- the summaries of findings from the inspection and review process relating to the publication of reports on individual establishments and services across all sectors over the last five, four or three years, depending on the sector involved*;

- the findings from inspections of educational establishments contributing to the production of aspect reports across all sectors, and HMIE commentary on those findings as published in such aspects reports;

- information drawn from surveys (for example of stakeholders' views on inspection);

- reflections on the basis of ongoing interactions with a very broad range of key players in the education process (such as Scottish Executive staff, Directors of Education and other local authority personnel, staff from other education agencies, headteachers, principals, teaching and non-teaching staff, researchers and others involved in higher education);

- reflections on the basis of discussions both internal to HMIE and involving others taking part in inspection processes such as associate assessors, lay members, representatives of agencies engaged in joint inspections (such as the Care Commission, or Audit Scotland); and

- HM Inspectors' knowledge in terms of research findings, theory and provision in relevant sectors and in specific contexts.

* Inspection details as follows:

pre-school:	1602 inspections undertaken jointly with the Care Commission, 2003-2005
primary:	633 inspections, including independent sector provision, 2002-2005
secondary:	136 inspections, including independent sector provision, 2002-2005
special:	35 inspections of day schools, including ten for pupils with social, emotional and behavioural difficulties, 2002-2005
	36 inspections of residential schools, including independent sector provision, 2002-2005
college:	46 inspections, incorporating 306 subject areas, 2000-2004
CLD:	inspections of geographical areas in 30 local authorities, 2002-2005.

Further details

Further details on many aspects reported on in this report are available in HMIE reports or from the HMIE website (**www.hmie.gov.uk**). Publications are listed in the Reference and Bibliography Appendix associated with this report on the website. Of particular interest may be the reports on:

- the findings of the first cycle of inspections of the education functions of local authorities;

- the findings of the first cycle of inspections of Community Learning and Development across all local authorities; and

- the annual analysis of college reviews of each year and an overview of findings across all years of the review cycle to date.

Use of terms

Terms describing people

- **'parent/s'** should be understood as including foster carers, residential care staff and carers who are relatives or friends. It should also be understood as referring to one or two (or more) adults in the parent role

- **'learner'** is used generically to refer to school pupils, young people in college, or young people or adults in the community learning and development (CLD) context. The word **'participant'** is also used in the CLD context, where the word 'learner' may not be so appropriate

- **'young people'** is used to refer across any sector to that group of individuals aged around 14 to 18; occasionally the term is used in the 5 to 18 context

- **'pupil'** is used exclusively in the context of schools

- **'children'** is used in the pre-school context and in parent-children relational contexts

- **'teacher'** or **'teaching staff'** are used across all sectors to refer to those adults in teaching situations who have a teaching qualification

- **'non-teaching staff'** or **'support staff'** are used to refer to other adults in the teaching situation who support the teaching process. They may have a professional qualification. The term includes nursery nurses, nursery or classroom assistants, auxiliaries for children, pupils and young people with additional support needs, technicians, resource auxiliaries and others

- **'staff'** is used to cover both the above groups

- **'headteacher'** is used for school contexts and for nursery schools in the pre-school sector

- **'centre manager'** is used in the pre-school sector to refer to the person in overall charge in voluntary or private centres as relevant

- **'head'** is used generically to refer across all educational establishments and services

- **'senior staff'** or **'senior managers'** refers to senior promoted staff and may include the head, headteacher or centre manager

- **'inspectors'** relates to personnel engaged in inspections or reviews and includes HM Inspectors, associate assessors and other members of inspection or review teams

Qualitative and quantitative terms

The evaluative words: 'very good', 'good', 'fair' and 'unsatisfactory' are as associated with the four quality indicator levels in *How good is our school?* and in other sector inspection documentation, prior to the introduction of the six-point scale in August 2005. The levels are described as follows:

very good:	provision with major strengths;
good:	provision where strengths outweigh weaknesses;
fair:	provision with some important weaknesses;
unsatisfactory:	provision with major weaknesses.

The following standard terms of quantity are used in all HMIE reports:

All:	100%
Almost all:	90% – 99%
Most:	75% – 89%
Majority:	50% – 74%
A few:	less than 15%

Other quantitative terms which may be used in this report are to be understood as in common English usage.